D1029364

NORMAN LEWIS
THE TOMB IN SEVILLE

Crossing Spain on the Brink of Civil War

Introduction by
JULIAN EVANS

CARROLL & GRAF PUBLISHERS
NEW YORK

THE TOMB IN SEVILLE
Crossing Spain on the Brink of Civil War

Carroll & Graf Publishers
An Imprint of Avalon Publishing Group Inc.
245 West 17th Street
11th Floor
New York, NY 10011

AVALON
publishing group incorporated

Copyright © 2003 by the Estate of Norman Lewis
Introduction copyright © 2003 by Julian Evans

First Carroll & Graf edition 2005

Library of Congress Cataloging-in-Publication Data is available.

ISBN: 0-7867-1439-5

9 8 7 6 5 4 3 2 1

Printed in the United States of America
Distributed by Publishers Group West

INTRODUCTION

WRITERS ALIVE TO Spain's appeal in the Twenties and Thirties – that appeal that tragically mutated into a cry of pain – travelled there because Spain was Europe's antithesis: a fantastic landscape of hallucinations and extremes, of heat, human incongruity and implacable vitality. For Norman Lewis, it also represented escape from his own distinct version of northern European neurosis. In his first volume of autobiography, *Jackdaw Cake*, he describes his lower middle-class suburban background in Enfield, north London, as 'an endless, low-quality dream . . . nothing, with chips', and his struggle to wake up from that dream has an escapologist's wild vigour – motor racing, get-rich-quick business schemes (plagiarising foreign newspapers, selling umbrellas), a rash marriage to the daughter of a Sicilian man of honour. But Spain, significantly, is more than the place of his first flight: in a life compelled by the pull of the world, it is the place he returned to more often than any other, the temper with which he most identified. When, after 1945, he lived for three summers in a fishing village on what is now the Costa Brava, the happiness he experienced became his touchstone for the next half-century. Whenever his writing turns to Spain, as it does here again, something about his relationship with the country – not just his familiarity with it – seems to produce a distillation of his prose. That is saying a lot for a writer whose reputation rests extensively on his stylistic genius.

Lewis first travelled to Spain in the autumn of 1934. *Spanish Adventure*, the first book he published, relates a journey one hardly associates with the author of *A Dragon Apparent* and *Naples '44*: a planned voyage by canoe through the waterways of southern Europe.

'From the very first my attitude towards the canoe,' he writes, 'was tinged with distrust and condescension.'

This first sentence, straight from Peter Fleming or Robert Byron, gives the game away. *Spanish Adventure* is a derivative of the high-jinks or Wodehousian school of travel writing; Lewis himself quickly became conscious of its faults, suppressing mention of it when his first serious success, *A Dragon Apparent*, appeared in 1952, and ever after – although once when I stayed at his house in Finchingfield he lent me a copy, guaranteeing I would find paragraphs of hysterical prose on almost every page. Yet *Spanish Adventure* has plenty of felicities, like this description of the Navarran landscape:

a boundless plain of billowing rock, from which all colour has been purged by the sun, leaving a panorama empty of everything but whiteness of cloud and rock and the blue of the sky. Against such terrestrial purity one is demoted to the status of a stain.[†]

[†] Tiring of the canoe, Lewis and his companion Eugene – his Sicilian wife's brother – had rapidly abandoned it before entering Spain from France.

Most importantly, it relates a journey that stamped the future indelibly upon him. It touched, in Robert Louis Stevenson's phrase, 'a virginity of sense', and by its end he knew that he was not interested in doing anything but travelling and writing.

Norman Lewis's place today as the father of modern travel writing is unassailable. It is so because, among other things, he changed the category. Until the Second World War, British travel writers often blatantly did two jobs at once. The passes, deserts and rivers they conquered could be a personal triumph today, an imperial army's supply route tomorrow. The Royal Geographical Society in Kensington Gore boasted more colonels than a junta. But he was one of the first writers to travel in a spirit of pure fascination, spurred on by his belief that 'the next valley would always be wilder'. He taught many other writers their craft, though none achieved his degree of self-erasure. To read him – his sensuous and civilised descriptions, his poker-faced wit, his anecdotal genius for painting the world's beauty and humanity's routine disarray – is to fall under the spell of a prose whose magic is embedded in his youthful reading: the King James Bible, Herodotus, Suetonius, and the Russian novels in Enfield Library. 'As I never had the chance to read rubbish,' he said once, 'I couldn't absorb the rubbish which went with the style of the popular writers.'

Though he is conventionally called a travel writer, Norman Lewis's books are not travel books in what I think of as the 'orientalist' sense – in which successive cults for representing the exotic dominate what we know of the world. Lewis was no orientalist (although in the other sense of that word, he knew South-East Asia like no other writer I have read); he was more accurately a witness, a reconstructor. Eric Hobsbawm, almost Lewis's contemporary, has remarked that our accelerated culture is destroying the mechanism of historical memory that links each generation's experience to that of earlier generations. Lewis was one of the greatest of those links. Though the world is more global than it was in the eighteenth century, it is not incongruous to see him as Defoe's heir, or Fielding's or Cobbett's.

Norman Lewis was ninety-five when he died in July 2003. In his last decade he published a string of books which would have been prolific for a writer half his age: *An Empire of the East*, about his travels through Indonesia; *The World, The World*, a second volume of autobiography; *In Sicily*, about his return to that haunted island; and two collections of articles, *The Happy Ant-Heap* and *A Voyage by Dhow*. He had also had it in mind for some time, for personal reasons – including his children's desire to read the story – to revisit the Spain of that first adventure. *The Tomb in Seville*, his last book, is the result.

The bones of the story are the same as *Spanish Adventure*: a journey that takes Lewis and his brother-in-law first to Madrid and the bloody insurrection of October 1934, and then, via the length of Portugal, to Seville. There are two superficial differences, one in the method – no canoes – the other in the chronology. In *Spanish Adventure* Lewis goes on to north Africa; where the earlier book wanders from France and into Spain and out again, often submerged in hedonistic escapism, in *The Tomb in Seville* a quest has been identified, to be revealed, finally, and with due bathos, in the marvellous city of Seville.

That quest is also part of the deeper difference between the two books, embodied in a huge contrast of experience and language, in which the events of the journey, with their dramatic midpoint in the Madrid uprising, are reviewed and restored here. *The Tomb in Seville* is therefore really a double reconstruction: of a journey, and of a memory of a journey – a journey twice-distilled, in which the reader sees the purest version of that antithetical Spain I mentioned, the Spain of Lorca and Albéniz and the politician Antonio Cánovas del Castillo, who said of his people, '*Todo decae con frecuencia en España, menos la raza*' – 'Everything decays in Spain, except the race.'

In *The Tomb in Seville* Lewis's family connection with Spain is restored, too. His father-in-law, Ernesto Corvaja, was Sicilian, but of Andalusian stock, and it is in the pursuit of the Corvaja family's traces in Seville that Norman and his brother-in-law set out. Various states of alarm, announced by the government to aid their suppression of Communist unrest, prevent the travellers' smooth advance: at one point they are forced to walk the 110 miles to Zaragoza. As they arrive on the outskirts of the city, leaving the country behind, they get an inkling of another clash, not between government and Reds, but between the two Spains, past and future. '[We] set out on the last miles of the long trudge with the towers of Zaragoza, strangely Muscovite at that distance, finally jutting out of the horizon. Slowly the last of the hamlets fell behind and shrank in the distance. They had remained in their isolation here part of the Spain of the past, dignified in their poverty and uneasy with progress.'

It is here that he shows his preference, not just for Spain but for a Spain that precurses the twentieth century. 'Old Spain was a country of white cities, but Zaragoza's outline was dark.' What Lewis instinctively prefers is Moorish Spain, pre-industrial Spain, the Spain on the edge of Africa. In Zaragoza he alights on the rich, visible in quantity in their Rolls-Royces, with a certain distaste; Madrid under fire he describes as 'a weird and complicated child's toy'. You sense his reluctance towards cities, though Madrid's gun battles draw him like a magnet and he takes a terrific pleasure in details like the remark of a Cuban bar owner in Atocha, veteran of half a dozen revolutions, who approvingly explains that the police 'made a point of doing their best not to shoot a man in the cobblers'. Once out of the capital, his taste for the spectacular emptiness of plains and mountains immediately revives. This partiality for landscape is specific: the lushness of Portugal through which he and Eugene are forced to divert elicits a kind of scorn, 'the first vines and cabbages' unable to match the magnificence of 'the golden steppes' they have left, and produces a mild depression that only dissipates as they approach Seville and their goal.

The Tomb in Seville is a story of Spain come full circle. It is a feat not only of remembrance, but of reliving. Spain provides for Lewis, as it has done before, a perfect subject – and it occurs to me that it may be because he carried this extraordinary first journey in his memory for so long that his love of the country remained so strong. So Spain is not merely a subject here. It is a pole, a magnetic South to which the writer has been drawn, again, this time to produce both a work of restoration to delight in, and a fundamental explanation of why it draws him. The result is a story as distant as elegy, and more immediate than the news. That it comes from a writer in his tenth decade only increases the poignancy of his returning to the same ground (almost) as his first book, published nearly seventy years ago. As if, in going back to the roots of his writing career, he was setting out again in search of that irrecoverable beginning, when his impressions of the world had all the intoxicant vitality of newness.

Julian Evans
August 2003

CHAPTER 1

MY FATHER-IN-LAW, Ernesto Corvaja, although Sicilian by birth, was obsessively concerned with all matters pertaining to Spain. His family originally came from there, which was evident from their name, and there was said to be evidence to prove that an ancestor had been included in the suite of the viceroy Caracciolo, sent from Spain to Sicily following its conquest.

In his London house Ernesto still nourished the ghost of a Spanish environment with a housekeeper recruited from some sad Andalusian village who glided silently from room to room wearing a skirt reaching to her ankles, and kept the house saturated with the odour of frying saffron. Despite Ernesto's agnosticism, a Spanish priest in exile was called in to bless the table on the days of religious feasts, and although Ernesto's son Eugene resisted his father's efforts to send him to Spain to complete his studies, his daughter, Ernestina, briefly to be my wife, had agreed to spend a year in a college in Seville.

Visits to Spain had taken on the nature of quasi-religious pilgrimages in this household, and Eugene's resistance was finally overcome by his father's offer to pay the expenses both of my brother-in-law and myself for a visit of two months to Seville. Here we could inspect the remains of the old so-called Corvaja Palace, pay our respects at the family tomb in the cathedral, and discover if any memory, however faint, had survived of the Corvajas in the ancient capital of Andalusia.

Our Spanish travels, it was decided, would begin at San Sebastián, just across the country's north-western frontier with France, thereafter following a slightly more circuitous approach to Seville, through the less developed and, to us, more interesting areas, including in the west, for example, the towns of Salamanca and Valladolid.

On Sunday 23 September 1934 we attempted to book seats on the train for San Sebastián, only to be told at the London ticket office that bookings could be made only as far as Irun on the French frontier with Spain. Here a temporary interruption of the traffic was expected to be rectified next day.

At Irun some twenty hours later, we found the frontier closed and the air buzzing with rumours; several Spanish passengers showed signs of alarm. Nevertheless those with tickets for Salamanca were given accommodation in a small but excellent local hotel, and a guide was provided to show us round a somewhat unexciting town. In the morning, entry into Spain had been restored and we boarded a train which carried us through to San Sebastián in just over a half-hour.

In a way the hold-up at the frontier had been interesting for us, providing an instant and striking demonstration of the contrasts in style and character of the two peoples involved. Irun was full of alert and energetic Frenchmen and women who made no concession to the southern climate, rose early to plunge into their daily tasks, ate and drank sparingly at midday and in the early evening, fore-gathered socially thereafter for an hour or two before retiring to a splendid coffee-scented bar. This, we were to discover, was the diametric opposite of the Spanish way of life. The French lived in a kind of nervous activity. They hastened from one engagement to another with an eye kept on their enormous clocks.

To arrive in San Sebastián, a few miles across the frontier, was to be plunged into a different world. This was a town of white walls guarding the privacy of its citizens, all such surfaces being covered with huge political graffiti. No one was in a hurry, or carried a parcel, and here there were no clocks. Irun's restaurants filled for the midday meal at 12.30 p.m. and emptied one hour later, when their patrons returned to their offices or shops. Those of San Sebastián admitted their first customers at 2 p.m., and these would have spent an absolute minimum of an hour and a half over the meal before vacating their tables. The majority then returned home for a siesta of an hour or so before tackling their afternoon's work.

'How long do you suppose we'll be staying?' Eugene asked.

'Well, two or three days, I'd say. What do you think? It's more interesting than I expected. I was talking to the chap who does the rooms. San Sebastián is famous for its *paseos* apparently. You know what a *paseo* is?'

'Well, more or less.'

'Most old-fashioned towns have one. Here they have two – a popular version for the working class in the early evening and a select one, as they call it, for the better people later on. I read somewhere they haven't scrapped the *piropo* here.'

'The what?'

'The *piropo*. The habit of shouting sexually offensive remarks at good-looking women in the *paseo* – or even in the street. The dictator Primo de Rivera put a stop to it, but it's crept back into favour again in places like this.'

'Right then,' said Eugene, 'let's make it three days.'

The Royalty Hotel seemed to reflect the old style of life, and was full of what Eugene described as bowing and scraping.

'What comes after this?' he wanted to know.

'Well, Burgos I suppose. Nice comfortable distance. About seventy or eighty miles. With a good car we could do it in the morning, or carry on to Valladolid which sounds more interesting. Pity nothing's said about the state of the roads.'

'They'll be able to tell us at the hotel, I'm sure.'

The four-course dinner took us by surprise, but we did our best with the huge portions. Eugene went off to give Ernesto a surprise phone call, but came back shaking his head. 'No lines through to England at the moment,' he said. The people in the hotel all seemed surprised.

Later that day Eugene received a surprise request from the woman who had waited on us at table, and had received our compliments in the matters of service and food with obvious pleasure. Her request was that one or the other of us would escort her in the first *paseo* that evening. Such was the prestige in San Sebastián, she explained, of foreign visitors from the north, that to appear in public with one infallibly enhanced a local girl's status. Dorotea was both pretty and exceedingly charming, so her request was immediately granted. Eugene provided a splendid bouquet and we then spent the hour and a half of the *paseo* strolling girl in arm in the company of several hundred local citizens in the formal gardens by the sea.

The *paseo* was accepted as health-giving, rejuvenating exercise. More importantly, for the traveller out of his

4

depth in foreign surroundings and reduced to constant apology and confusion imposed by the loss of language, it was a godsend. Whether merchant, soldier or minister of religion, the *paseo* smoothed out all the problems. The mere act of walking in the company of beaming strangers provoked a change of mood. Within minutes of joining a *paseo*'s ranks the beginner had shaken hands with everyone in sight – a cordial gripping of fists sometimes strong enough to produce a moistening of the eyes. The leaflet we collected as new members of the 'friendly walk' advised us that one should 'always smile, but laugh with caution'. A number of actions came under its ban: 'At all times refrain from shouting or whistling. Gestures with the fingers are to be avoided. Do not wink, do not turn your back on a bore in an ostentatious manner, and, above all, never spit.'

From Eugene's viewpoint the experience turned out to be so attractive that he was a little sad when it was at an end. We were to learn next day that even the hotel approved of this adventure on the part of a member of the staff. 'The manager complimented me,' Dorotea said. 'They hope to be able to give me an increase in salary next spring.'

Eugene tried to ring home again, but all international lines were still engaged. The manager seemed to find this as baffling as we did. Purely for a change of scene we hired a car and set off to drive a mile or two along the coast road to France. We didn't get very far before we were stopped by two Civil Guards who had left their car to stretch white tape across the road. They were typical of their kind, grey of jowl and verging on middle age. These must have been the last survivors in San Sebastián of the old-fashioned military police. Otherwise the municipality had already been able to import several of the smart new Assault Guards. It was made clear to us that the road back to France was closed.

'Why so many coppers?' I wondered aloud to Eugene. 'Surely not another revolution on the way?'

'You never know,' he said. 'After all this *is* Spain. Anyway, what'll we do tonight?'

I told him I'd spotted a cabaret at the end of the main street. 'Probably be a bit of a fake, but it'll use up some time,' I said.

We had dinner at the hotel, where Dorotea was full of smiles, and after that we made for the cabaret which, said a notice scrawled in chalk on the door, was shut for that evening, 'owing to circumstances'. What on earth, we wondered, did they mean by that? You can't get through on the telephone to a foreign country, the road to France is closed, and now the cabaret's decided to pack up for the night. Just what *is* happening? I wondered. 'Do you think perhaps we shouldn't have come here after all?'

When we returned to the hotel we found one of the grey, old Civil Guards at the reception desk. He asked us to note down our occupations, our religion, our reason for coming to Spain and how long we proposed to stay. We were finally instructed to present ourselves at nine the next morning at the barracks of the Civil Guard in order for photographs to be taken.

'I must admit,' said the hotel manager, 'that this has been an experience a foreign guest is bound to find alarming. However an explanation from the police is bound to be forthcoming, and I am sure that the rest of your stay with us will be trouble-free in every way.'

We agreed, not least because San Sebastián appeared to us as a town well adjusted to the calmer routine of urban life. That evening Dorotea and a friend joined us on the fashionable *paseo*. Parting company with them at about ten, we were delighted to discover that the cabaret had opened after all, and so spent an hour there listening to *cante flamenco* before going to bed.

Next morning, Friday 28 September, an official State of Alarm was declared throughout Spain. The announcement, broadcast on the radio at 6 a.m., and subsequently repeated at half-hour intervals, warned the population of the curtailment of certain civil liberties, the imposition of a curfew at 9 p.m., and of restrictions upon travel. Further local information would be made available at all *municipios*. After a brief discussion, Eugene and I agreed that our best hope would be to pay our bills and get down to the station as soon as we could in the hope of seats on the morning train to the south. But when we got there we found that the Civil Guards we had seen on the previous day had used their car to close off the entrance to the station. They told us that not only would there be no train to Seville, but that no train at all would be leaving for any destination in the country on this day.

Turning back to make for the centre, we were suddenly both to experience a sensation that the personality of this town had undergone a remarkable change. The people of San Sebastián, as we had agreed, seemed to set great store by matters of personal deportment. They held themselves erect, walked in a dignified manner and with no evidence of haste. This we attributed to some extent to a climate with summer temperatures that could be high. But it was also probably based upon remnants of a cultural inheritance from the Moors. At this moment San Sebastián seemed full of running figures and queues had formed at the doors of food shops with desperate would-be customers struggling to get in. Such was the confusion that even the *paseos* were abandoned.

As the day wore on the excitement and despair of the early hours were replaced by a growing lethargy as the public became acclimatised to a crisis that had never been explained. But what exactly was a State of Alarm, and why had one been declared? These were the questions the citizens of San Sebastián now demanded more insistently be answered, as indeed did I. Choosing a quiet spot in the gardens along the sea-front Eugene was ready with an explanation.

'Spain is on the verge of a civil war,' he said. 'I had a quiet chat with the manager while you were having your camera fixed, and he told me that the miners in Asturias have started a revolt.'

'And that's the State of Alarm?'

'No, that's only part of the thing. Listen, I should have told you before but I've been putting it off. I've joined the Communist Party, and apart from Ernesto's ridiculous pilgrimage idea, that's the reason I'm here.'

'You could have told me,' I said.

'Of course I should have. I kept putting it off.'

'Why?'

'I didn't know how you'd take it.'

'It's a pity you didn't. We've known each other long enough for me not to give a damn what party you join. Anyway communism is only one of the modern religions. Trouble is, I'm not a believer.'

There was a moment of silence. 'But listen,' I said. 'Do you really believe this country's going to go Red?'

'I'm certain of it.'

'They won't,' I said. 'The Spanish are individualists to a man. You'll not catch them turning into a bunch of fanatics,' I assured him. 'I know them too well, and you should too.'

'Anyway we'll soon see,' Eugene said.

Where did he pick up this bout of fanaticism, I asked myself, particularly with a father like Ernesto who had assured him in my presence that no Sicilian believed in anything?

'So when's it going to start?' I asked. 'The real thing. When is the man on the street – who's the one who really counts – going to throw out his chest and tell you he's a member of the party of Lenin?'

'Very soon,' Eugene assured me. 'A month – two months at most. You and I are going to be present at one of the great moments in history. I can't tell you how lucky we are to find ourselves here, waiting for the curtain to go up.'

'And where and when will that happen?'

'In Madrid, and probably today. By the way, the manager let it slip that the Asturian miners in Oviedo are already out fighting in the streets.'

'That's a couple of hundred miles away up in the north. Our problem now is how do we get to Madrid?'

'Well, naturally from here, or anywhere else, as soon as the trains start running again. The hotel people have been through all this before, and they say a week or two at most.'

'Just imagine another couple of weeks stuck in this place,' I said.

The fact was that neither Eugene nor I had any idea of what manipulations the Spanish politicians and the military were conducting behind the scenes. The present situation, in which an official State of Alarm could impose near-paralysis upon the public, had largely arisen through brusque and unexpected changes of direction in the corridors of power. From 1923 to 1930 Spain had suffered under the almost medieval dictatorship of Primo de Rivera. When he fell there had been a political swing to the opposite extreme and the Second Republic was established, practising liberalism in an extreme form. For the first time women were given the vote. Little could the legislators of the day have imagined that far from pressing for more liberal reforms, women would instead come to the aid of the powers of reaction. This, however, they did, and a new feminine alliance was formed to clear Spain of politicians with liberal ideas. It was from this climate, with women close to political control, that such measures as the State of Alarm were frequently in use, and battles, as we were to discover, could be fought even on the streets of Madrid.

CHAPTER 2

THE HOTEL MANAGER, Enrico, seemed to have taken a liking to us, and with time on his hands, due to the State of Alarm emptying three-quarters of his rooms, he was happy to conduct us round the formal gardens known as La Concha. These were normally out of bounds to members of the male sex for several hours during the day. This, he explained, was to protect the privacy of several hundred wet nurses who, with their charges held to their bosoms, took over the more secluded areas of the park in the early afternoon. Enrico timed the operation like a military manoeuvre, enabling us to slip in and out of the cover of the hedges and remain uninvolved. Screened as we were among the leaves, not an eye appeared to have been raised in our direction as rows of mammae on all sides were unslung and then, with drill-like precision, duly put away.

The wet nurses were followed at a discreet distance by a horde of young children with their attendant servants. The servants, Enrico told us, were all Basques, tall and muscular young fellows, dressed, in order not to be confused with visitors, in uniforms displaying fashions of the last century. These included pigtails tied with immense bows and shirts with leg o'mutton sleeves. When on rare occasions – usually by mistake – ordinary visitors happened to wander into these secluded areas at this busy hour, these servants were trained to greet them with welcoming smiles and low bows.

Enrico had invented a new attraction for the town's visitors. He employed pigtail-wearing servants from La Concha, dressed in their nineteenth-century livery as before, but also carrying lanterns, to accompany hotel guests on sight-seeing tours of the town by night. It was a project, however, that lost business and had to be abandoned.

I cornered Enrico again. 'Can you think of any way out of here? Even if we could get only a few miles along the road to Seville it would be something.'

'But you'd never do it,' he said. 'The only place you might be able to get to from here is Pamplona.'

'It's in the wrong direction,' I pointed out.

'It's in the *only* direction. You wouldn't get a mile along the Seville highway. Pamplona's on a side road.'

'But why Pamplona? What's it got to offer?'

'Its insignificance. It's the old Spain. Something out of the past. Nobody bothers about the place. They won't even notice you're there. Be polite to the old people and buy the kids a few sweets. The place is run by a sergeant in the Civil Guard. He's fifty-eight and gets all the sleep he can. In Pamplona they still bury people standing upright. About twenty or thirty families live in caves.'

'How does going to Pamplona help us get to Seville?' I wanted to know.

'Well at the moment it doesn't,' Enrico said, 'but it's the sort of place where it's easy to make yourself liked, which means that if they can do anything for you they will. And that includes finding some way of getting to Seville.'

'Doesn't the State of Alarm bother them?'

'No way of knowing, but if it does I'd guess the pressure is a lot less than in San Sebastián.'

A van with an official pass stuck on the windscreen was delivering meat to Pamplona that afternoon. 'So why not take a chance?' Enrico suggested. 'You've nothing to lose. The police have got plenty to keep them occupied just now without bothering about you.' The van was parked in a street at the back of the hotel and the driver looked in the other direction while we pulled up the flap at the back and clambered in.

The road took us through pleasantly mountainous countryside dotted with wooden houses, half extinguished, in the Tyrolean fashion, by their eaves. Beauty was once again under the protection of poverty. There was no money about, the driver said, as we bumped along round the holes as deep as baths that kept the tourists away. An eagle, tearing at some small carcass, waited until we were within fifteen yards before spreading its wings to take to the air. Where there are eagles, the driver said, men go short of bread.

Behind this desolate beauty the outline of Pamplona raised itself cautiously from among low hills and I was at first delighted by the town's mouldering ramparts but then almost immediately discouraged as an area of industrial development came into sight. What do they produce in the heart of this amphitheatre of nature, I asked, and the reply was bathroom fittings and sanitary appliances. While old Pamplona guarded its silences, the new town uttered a muffled roar of profitable activity. Understandably there were no tourists in sight, for Pamplona, we were to learn, possessed just one hotel. The Montaña charged eight pesetas fifty centimos a day – the equivalent of six shillings and nine pence for full board, and naturally enough, said the manageress, wine was included with both meals.

We were already well aware of the fact that such cheap Spanish hotels, however little they charged, always did their best to give a lot for the money. Thus, instead of concentrating on simple two-course meals based on wholesome materials, they insisted on performing feats of camouflage with what was left over and bought at auctions in the markets at the end of the day's business, and in serving it up in four or five often abominable courses.

The Montaña offered the finest example of this competitive policy in action that one could hope to find; both ingenuity and imagination were employed in the processes of substitution and falsification of what was on offer. The tang of corruption was suppressed as far as possible by wholesale use of garlic. All cooking was done in the cheapest of rancid oil promoting odours that wandered through the building for an hour or so before and after each mealtime. This was to remind me that one of the charges on the indictment drawn up by the Inquisition leading to the expulsion of the Spanish Jews was that (to the offence of Christian nostrils) they cooked in oil.

Falsifications generally employed in such low-cost establishments were common throughout Spain in those days. It seemed extraordinary that the counterfeiters of food went to the lengths they did. There were even occasions in restaurants when we were confronted with such wild impostures as a fish described as a salmon but possessing the three-cornered spine of a conger eel or a small shark.

*　　*　　*

Among the small surprises of the Montaña Hotel was the news that its manageress was an ardent communist who organised the many political rallies taking place in the central square. Her husband, a mason, was employed at five pesetas (three shillings) a day on the building of a giant seminary just outside the town. He supplemented his wages, she told us with some pride, by producing busts of Lenin which commanded a good sale as household ornaments, replacing the biblical figures of old among the working class.

Eugene produced his membership card and we were invited to a cell meeting at which the prospects for the success of the coming revolution were discussed. At this time the armed revolt by Asturian miners was in full swing, with even such government newspapers as the *ABC* reporting with misgivings the slaughter produced by the shock troops employed to quell the revolt. Pamplona's communists had gone to the trouble of bringing down a miner to talk to them – a near dwarf whose ancestors had worked underground for generations. He convinced them with splendid oratory that the victory of socialism was at hand. Next day we were to discover that government censorship had suppressed all news from the north on the eve of a final battle in which tanks were in action against strikers armed with pickaxes, and a victory, never in doubt, was proclaimed.

Our State of Alarm problem refused to go away. In Pamplona we faced increasing difficulties through the frequent changes in and misunderstandings of the regulations applied to travel. All public transport in the Pamplona area remained at a standstill, in addition to which there were differences of opinion as to whether it was permissible or even safe to use private cars. This led to a delay in the supply of provisions to the towns, long queues at the food stores, and even their temporary closure.

Then news filtered through that although at first depressing, seemed to Eugene on second thoughts to offer a glimmer of hope. We were assured by one of the communists who had connections in Zaragoza that the only train in service in the country at that time was based in that town, and that it connected solely with Madrid. The capital was not quite halfway to Seville, but even to get so far as this on our journey offered hope of escape from our present frustrations. But how were we to reach Zaragoza? Such was the effectiveness of the State of Alarm in the Pamplona area it appeared that the last private cars had disappeared from the road.

One of the comrades suggested that we should simply walk there, the distance being a matter of about a hundred and ten miles and – as they assured us – it was a journey that had been done many times in the past. It was a solution, we decided, at least to be contemplated, and with the possibility, we hoped, of toughening ourselves we undertook what for us at that stage were several fairly strenuous lung-expanding walks into the surrounding countryside.

Finally, assuring ourselves that we had nothing to lose, we took the plunge. In a way we were unlucky due to the fact that after a long and exceptionally dry summer the rains had now started and the unsurfaced road to which we had committed ourselves, in a mistaken hope of shortening the distances involved, was soon to be deep in puddles. Fortunately the rain stopped, although it was to start again in a few hours, and we were able to take refuge and dry ourselves in the first of the few cafés to be encountered in the course of the journey. A remarkable feature of this small village, and several others to follow, was its possession of a church large enough for a medium-sized town, but even more singular was that its main tower appeared to serve as a lookout post over the surrounding countryside. It also had a small bell-tower for the transmission of simple messages. Thus, when after a few minutes we continued our walk, the bells were rung, and this peal appeared to have been answered by bell-ringing in the tower of the next church some three miles along the road. It was a method of communication to be followed from village to village the next day.

Happily, with the first two settlements behind us, and a sudden change in the weather, the rich gilding of summer returned to the Navarran landscape. It was Navarra that first confronted us with the splendour, the magnitude and even the mystery of these Spanish landscapes, which for many miles into the countryside round Pamplona offered the charm and the delicacy of a Chinese painting on silk. We moved across boundless plains of billowing rock purged of all colour by the sun. Distant clumps of poplar seemed to have been drawn up into the base of the sky in an atmosphere of mirage and mist. Behind the mountains ahead luminous and symmetrical clouds were poised without shift of position as we trudged towards them for hours on end. At our approach an anomalous yellow bloom shook itself from a single tree, transformed into a flock of green singing finches. Lizards, basking in the dust, came suddenly to life and streaked away into the undergrowth.

Our road crossed and recrossed the river in which vipers by the dozen were corkscrewing their way through the warm sunny water, and under a bridge of wooden planks we counted seven of them. An eagle detached itself from a boulder and flapped away towards the mountains. It was on a smooth rock face that an obituary was carved: 'Beneath this rock died Tomàs, "The Mule". June 8th 1916.' We wondered how Tomàs had come to earn his reputation for pig-headedness, and how this spot had been selected for his death, and whether his passing had been peaceful or violent.

The afternoon was well advanced before we stumbled into a hamlet where bread and wine was to be bought. What was more to the point was that the owner of a pioneer model Morris Cowley lived here and was proud of a chance to demonstrate the machine in action. Although the lights could not be switched on, in the gathering dusk he drove us determinedly and in defiance of the State of Alarm half the way to the next village.

We had already seen examples of humans living in caves within a few miles of San Sebastián, but it was here that we encountered the first of the true cave-dwellers of our days. These could have been villagers in cottages which through an earthquake of exceptional violence had toppled into holes in the earth from which roofs, chimneys, and even a window sometimes appeared. But on second glance they were obviously still too tidy to have survived a catastrophe. It was merely a matter of caves being rent-free and cool in summer as these were. And that, we were told, was the reason why in this area of Spain carefully planned and constructed caves were multiplying more rapidly than houses in many small villages.

We were to see many more of them a day later when, maps carefully studied then stuffed away in haversacks, we began the remaining miles to Zaragoza with only the vaguest idea of when we were likely to arrive. This, after all, we consoled ourselves, was accepted as a main road, and although it appeared to pass for the most part through isolated communities, there were many of them in which, if necessary, we could take refuge. Amazingly, so late in the year, the sun shone as brilliantly as ever on this vast plain with the soft inflation of the distances by the heat, and that morning Tiebas, Tores, and Carascai came successively into sight, afloat in the mist over the yellow earth.

How did their people live? Small men with ancestors who for a thousand years had fitted themselves into the cramped living spaces in this barren immensity, watched us from the roadside, avid perhaps for human company of any kind. A lean fox scrutinised us from its hole, a gaunt bush suddenly exploded with a hundred twittering birds, while small white butterflies had settled on nearby rocks like hoarfrost. Ringing bells were in our ears for the first two days of the long walk to Zaragoza. We would arrive in a village to find three or four young men waiting at the church doors who did no more than stare with no reply to our salutations. Once again we were to suspect that what we saw here was an ancient form of defensive drill against foreign invaders or even casual marauders. We were watched, it was evident, until we were out of sight when the bell-ringing was renewed. About midday we were relieved by the sight of a village shack calling itself a casino, with bread and salt to offer the traveller and jugfuls of thin white wine. In our unjustified ignorance we had failed to take into account the Spanish taboo against wearing shorts other than on sporting occasions, and a law still imposed in many rural communities ruled that, even in the case of males, the kneecaps must be covered. Tactfully reminded of this in the casino we hastened to put the matter right.

I saw Eugene as a lover of the natural world and believed that it was only his father's insistent championing of what he called 'real life' (largely to be measured in terms of financial prestige) that had so far debarred him from a career devoted to the great outdoors. Thus, although Ernesto himself was not to understand the mistake he had made in promoting our venture, it was inevitably to lead to an involvement with the Spain of the far past which otherwise neither of us would have experienced. As it was, much of our journey to Zaragoza was through hardly-trodden – and thus unspoiled – forest areas, and the wildlife observed on the walk was likely to be unusual if not unique in these surroundings.

On the night of the third day's walk we found ourselves in an area with no signs of human occupation, and were therefore relieved to sight what appeared to be a deserted cave a hundred yards or so off the road. After a previous night of mist and rain, and under what was still a doubtful sky, we climbed the hillside to consider the possibilities of sleeping there. We found that the ferns and other vegetation had been cleared away, and the cave itself appeared at first sight to be a pit, largely encircled by a low white-washed wall. The remnants of a door covered parts of a black opening and some effort was called for to tug the decayed door away and let in the light. This revealed a spacious cell with smooth walls upon which traces remained here and there of what might have been intricate paintings. Having studied these we moved on to explore a tunnel which proved to be only four or five yards in depth. Back in the stronger light several animal footprints were visible on the sandy floor. The most exciting discovery was what appeared to be part of a prehistoric pot sticking out of the wall.

We were about to settle down for the night here when Eugene spotted what he thought was a scorpion, which instantly took refuge in a crevice. This experience, plus the presence of a number of unidentifiable smaller insects – some brandishing what might have been stings in the rear ends of their bodies – caused us to change our minds of spending the night here, and to sleep in the open after all.

We awoke with the field lightly dusted with dawn and the squeaking of the first tree pipits in the branches above. An investigation into the possibilities of breakfast led us through various small villages of the neighbourhood, some consisting of as few as a dozen families living in houses with no more than two tiny rooms. The inhabitants were outstandingly similar to each other in their appearance. They were all remarkably short, although of sturdy appearance. There was something slightly alien about their full lips and flattened noses. Here there were no signs of the shyness we had experienced in some of the more northern villages. They laughed easily and accompanied a fluent conversation with excited gesticulation. Eugene speculated on the possibility of their being descendants of captives taken in the African wars of old. It was an interesting thought.

Above all they were exceedingly hospitable, and insisted on our staying in one of their cell-like rooms for the night. We were thankful for having brought children's toys with us for dispensation in situations such as this.

CHAPTER 3

SUDDENLY, FOUR HARD days' walk from our destination, we were plunged into a change of climate, and the cold, winter-scented rains were upon us. It had been a long, dry summer, but now the sky was dimpled with soft lilac clouds and we found ourselves trudging through new sharp-edged grass oozing water and watery odours. The young men here wore the locks of childhood, soon to be replaced, with the disappearance of adolescence, by cropped hair covered with caps in deference to the coming of winter. We slept in a cave for the first time, only for it to be invaded by huge frogs seeking to pack themselves in the mud. Later we were awakened by the whinings of what we took to be a wild dog that had found its way in, although we were later assured that this would certainly have been a local domestic variety, which having been lost or abandoned had adjusted to life in the wild.

By the next day steady rainfall had produced streams on both sides of the road, and these contained innumerable tiny fish darting here and there in a few inches of water. Following advice we had bought a couple of small circular nets and managed in the end to catch a dozen or so tiddlers between two and three inches in length. A hundred yards or so away, wading birds with long legs and necks had been added to the landscape and we studied their fishing methods and results with envy.

The quest for undisturbed sleep was only a partial success. Dawn brought the astonishing discovery that the long night of rainfall had produced a remarkable effect: stepping out into the morning light, we discovered that our stream had become a shallow river in which ducks were already prospecting for eels.

Quite suddenly the rainforest was upon us – a conclusive black line drawn across the horizon at the limit of the rusty pastures of summer. With this came almost instantaneous change. The birds of prey began to leave the sky. More importantly we were relieved of a plague of flies, and a few hours later we entered a different world for which Eugene had prepared himself with a series of slim paperbacks chiefly upon animal life, although flora of the rarer kind also came in for mention.

I joined him in his enthusiasm and blessed the good luck that had brought us here where we hoped not only to explore the wonders of nature but, in the cooler climate, to enjoy the arrival of the autumn rains. Here, then, we were confronted by a forest storehouse of the treasures of the natural world, untouched by civilisation. The magnificent forest trees were too far from the nearest town for them to be seen as valuable timber, and Spain's national universities considered themselves too poor to be able to finance academic tours dealing with natural history. Thus a treasure house of rare trees and plants had been left inviolate for investigation and enjoyment.

I discovered that Eugene had actually packed a small extensible butterfly net of the kind, he said, used by museum curators. The morning after our arrival a great sulphur-coloured butterfly failed to escape a swipe with this and was held for further inspection before release.

The next section of the rainforest was different in every way except the density of the arboreal growth. This was divided surprisingly between oaks and species of conifer. A covey of partridges circled the area while we were there, beating the air with stiff wings. We listened to a quick shuffle of small animals in a central thicket in which a splendid variety of the arum lily displayed a triumph in perpetual twilight. This indubitably was a rainforest, for a slow, steady rainfall fell all the time we were there. Eugene was happy to collect a snail that had purplish markings and was the size of a fist. A few dark moths changed direction to inspect us as they passed and we were treated to our first and probably last vision of that magnificent butterfly, the Purple Emperor – native almost exclusively of the oak-woods of southern Europe.

Yet another section of the forest was to take us by surprise. We climbed a slope up to a rampart of trees to be confronted with a black still-life of vegetation, dead to the eye. Here there were vast oaks set out by nature in their ranks and semicircles, lifted by centuries-old accumulation of leaf mould at their base to a kind of regal eminence over recent arboreal growth. The surrounding odour was one of sharp decay and an unchallenged antiquity bolstered by silence. Eugene noted down aproximate measurements, pacing out the distances between trunks. They were smooth, as if lightly polished, all reaching – he estimated – a height of about thirty-five feet. Holes made by woodpeckers were present in most cases about twenty feet from the ground – the area of trunk immediately below these entrances being whitened by the birds' droppings.

It was difficult not to be affected by this somewhat funereal environment, enlivened by the presence of many forms of attractive wildlife – the exotic birds, the spectacular butterflies and the extraordinary insects described in the illustrated booklets Eugene had included in his luggage. We were later to learn that this and other rainforests in the area were of special interest for the variety and exceptional size of their spiders. Their study had been wholly restricted to a few American scientists, and regarded as not of sufficient interest to the general public for books to be devoted to the subject, only one in fact having ever been published.

In the end our decision to spend a night in the rainforest was seen not only as a mild adventure but a closer association, however brief, with the greatest and most awe-inspiring of all living things, in the shade of which creatures of the jungle were puny indeed. Faced with these towering oaks that had grown from seeds no longer than fingernails to dominate their environment for centuries – or even a millennium – one was encouraged to speculate over the possible duration of life itself. Centuries of leaf-fall had covered the primeval terrain with a deep palliasse of leaf mould with which we made our beds. In the depths of this sounds suggestive of animal life were detected and were inevitably hostile to sleep. Eugene, whose hearing, as well as his capacity for belief, was better than mine, shovelled away at the leaf soil for an hour before putting his ear to the ground and then reporting a variety of sounds. He had read somewhere, he said, of colonies of prehistoric creatures collected and supported by trees in their deep roots.

High overhead a tide of birds had been swept in by the night, and began their sad hootings among the topmost branches. Until then we had heard little, the only sound being the clicking of stick insects hurrying along the twigs in search of their prey. Now there were only the owls to remind us of night.

Beyond the last of the forest next day we discovered a cautious return of the human presence. There were plots of cultivated land, some with the scrawny remains of the harvest of that year, and the first isolated settlement. Here we encountered a plea from a lonely man. 'We don't see anyone here for days on end. If you live in this place you long for the sight of a fresh face. Couldn't you stay a little and talk? I can't tell you how much we long to hear the latest news. Why not stay until tomorrow?'

The occupants of these tiny clusters of cottages lacked occupation and any form of creativity. Few crops could be induced to grow on this arid, sandy soil which normally supported little more than a kind of pampas grass. Such isolated communities were in the end bled dry, too, by the loss of the most energetic, intelligent and creative of their youngsters who were tempted to go in search of employ-ment in the great Rioja vineyards, a day's journey away to the west. Of those who went there in search of a new life, few wished to return.

The feudal overlords of this area were the owners of the vineyards who lived, according to our informants, in palatial mansions a day or so's horseback journey away. We were later to learn in Zaragoza that they liked, above all, to be considered patrons of the arts, and one had even written a book on the antiquities of the area, scattered largely through the fields. These had been moulded in some cases by ten thousand storms into more or less recognisable animal, or even human, shapes, and were collected by rich landowners who built them into the walls of their houses. The serf who found one might even be paid up to the equivalent of a year's wages for it.

Small, sluggish rivers trickled slowly in all directions across the plain, and cranes, carefully spaced out, possibly to avoid spoiling each other's catch, waited patiently with a taxidermic rigidity in the shallows. Fish, however, remained plentiful, and finding a shop with fishing tackle for sale we equipped ourselves with rods and lines, and were repaid with a few sizeable fish, rescuing us from semi-starvation.

The day's long walk offered a rare moment of luxury when we came to its end at Tafalla, which had a hotel with a bar and even, to our amazement, the ghost of a *paseo*, with several crestfallen girls awaiting an invitation to display their charms. Next morning we set out early but had to take refuge from the rain in the stark little village of Ujué – an almost unpronounceable name given it, we were told, by a nomadic tribe which finally established itself there a thousand or so years back.

No more settlements were shown in this area on the map, so we slept out uneasily, and were frequently disturbed by strange whining sounds in our vicinity. Could wild dogs possibly exist in Spain, we wondered. There was no reason to defer an early start, so we set off shortly after dawn, reaching Tudela in the early afternoon. This – the most extraordinary town either of us had ever seen – came into view across the river Ebro. It appeared at first to be composed entirely of cave dwellings, many of them very large. Later, after a brief exploration, I wrote in my notes that on first sight we estimated there were probably as many caves as normal houses.

We ran into a local man strolling with his dog on our side of the river who was happy to talk to us. He agreed that probably half the population were cave-dwellers, but since the caves were cooler in summer and warmer in winter he insisted that many families did so out of preference. There were, of course, economic advantages. Caves were bought, sold and rented precisely as normal houses were, although naturally at lower prices. The more complex caves were divided into several rooms: those in the neighbourhood of such towns as Zaragoza could be fitted with electric light and leased or sold by instalments or otherwise through the usual housing agents. They attracted little or no outside interest, he assured me. Many tourists, he said, came to Tudela, invariably in summer, to visit the local stork colony – one of the largest in Spain – and to photograph the immense nests built on the towers of the church.

With some difficulty we found a room in one of the smaller and simpler caves and were served an excellent meal in another which, through development, had become a miniature labyrinth.

A little nervous about the possibility of missing the train to Madrid, we reluctantly decided to abandon our plan to spend a further day in Tudela and to press on with all possible speed. We were therefore up at dawn in the absurd hope of reaching Zaragoza in a single day. The surrounding landscape, we were to find, had changed almost miraculously overnight and featureless plains were filling with uplands such as the Montes de Castagon from the crags of which a number of fishing eagles launched to investigate us as we passed. Whereas the plains had been almost as dry as a desert, here it had rained in the night, filling the air with damp autumnal scents. Plants of all kinds were waking from the long trance of summer, and wherever we looked small starry blooms popped up on the surface of the earth.

Approaching the banks of the river at Alargon, we passed

close to a group of piratical-looking fishermen in hooded capes and long boots wading in the shallows. Stopping for a moment to watch them we were astonished by the way they bowed their heads as if in prayer before casting in their lines. They were close enough for us to chat with a recent arrival before he splashed into the water. It had been a hot, dry summer, he said. This was the best time to fish. Particularly when the rain happened to coincide with a religious feast, when up to double the normal catch could be expected. Reminded that these were moveable feasts, he returned a happy laugh. 'It is of no importance. God's blessing comes with the feast, whether they move or not.'

Everywhere the night's rains had saturated the landscape through which we had been limping on sore feet. A final spurt would have brought us within reach of the suburbs of Zaragoza before dark, but we gradually realised that this was a forlorn hope and decided to stop at Casetas. This substantial village offered a *casa rural* with beds, and its owner, dressed as an American cowboy, rode up to guide us in. There was food and lodging of a kind, and that was all that mattered. It was hardly dark before we were asleep.

The cowboy wakened us with the first light, and insect-bitten, with raw skin and feet bandaged in our shoes, we set out on the last miles of the long trudge with the towers of Zaragoza, strangely Muscovite at that distance, finally jutting out of the horizon. Slowly the last of the hamlets fell behind and shrank in the distance. In their isolation they had remained part of the Spain of the past, dignified in their poverty and uneasy with progress. But as we had found, they were full of style, and we saw them as the successful human furniture of these sun-drenched plains backed by the distant sierras.

CHAPTER 4

OLD SPAIN WAS a country of white cities, but Zaragoza's outline was dark. For five days we had drawn the purest of air into our lungs, but even with three miles to go before we faced its suburbs we sniffed a sharp industrial scent. There was something about the intertwining syllables of this city's name that Eugene found oriental. And by what manoeuvre, we asked ourselves, could it be in this time of national crisis that the only travellers to the capital by train would be those boarding in Zaragoza?

We were now faced with a new experience, for this was one of Spain's leading industrial towns, priding itself in a modernity of outlook and style not to be outclassed anywhere in the country. We reached the first of the suburbs by the early afternoon, and were shortly passing the first of its many factories. We had walked a hundred-odd miles through landscapes scented by pastures, rivers, and even mists. Zaragoza, we were to decide, smelt of electricity.

We had been warned that we would find the town expensive and therefore set out to choose our lodgings with caution. By this time we had learned, too, that cheap accommodation was to be found on the outskirts of most Spanish towns – the furthest out from the centre being the cheapest – and here we contracted ourselves for a single night in the first hotel to come into sight. What was unusual about this particular hotel was that it did business under four different names: the Granadina, Oriente, Pilar and La Perla. It was Granadina over the door, Oriente on the form the porter handed me to fill in, the notices in the rooms referred to it as El Pilar, and the luncheon menu bore the name La Perla, while the crockery in use in the evening meal carried yet another name.

The Hotel Granadina bore evidence of having once been fashionable, but never was the approach of dissolution more evident. A whiff of change and decay lingered in all the public rooms. Chipped spittoons alternated with drooping palms along untrodden corridors. Our only fellow diner was a priest whose leanness, deeply melancholic eyes and choice of hotel marked him out as unsuccessful in his calling.

Zaragoza was a communist stronghold, which possibly was justifiable since I could not remember ever visiting a town in which poverty presented itself in so stark a contrast with wealth. The number of Rolls-Royces in its streets could only have been exceeded by those in the West End of London. The poor were engaged in such operations as sifting through rubbish bins and dumps, and in the worst possible cases even guarding the sewer mouths for the nameless garbage vomited at intervals into the river. Communist propaganda posters were abundantly on display.

Being a Party member Eugene considered it something of a duty to pay a call at the headquarters of the class struggle in such a politically-minded city, and we obtained the necessary address from the first person we stopped in the street and went there without delay. We were received by a charming lady secretary dressed in a garment suggesting a compromise between fashion and politics, and having registered his presence in the city Eugene took me aside to raise a question. Surely, he suggested, the moment had arrived for me to sign the book? I felt obliged to explain that I was not religious.

'Nor am I,' he said. 'Religion has nothing to do with this.'

'You're mistaken,' I told him.

I had discovered that the leaders of the faithful here called themselves '*rasouls*'. It was an Arabic word that had somehow survived in modern Spanish, meaning in Arabic 'disciples', although now translated as 'communists'.

I left Eugene at the Communist Party headquarters and went back to the hotel. When he returned it was with the exciting news that an armoured train would leave for Madrid at midday on the next day, and that he had been able to buy tickets. What, I asked, did he suppose was an armoured train? He replied that they had made some reference to the fact that it carried troops with heavy machine-guns, to defend the train if it came under attack.

At headquarters, Eugene had been allowed to attend a meeting in which the likelihood of an armed insurrection was considered, the general expectation being that this would take place in a matter of days. It had been reported from Madrid that minor skirmishing between communist shock troops and a company of the new Assault Guards had occurred in the outer suburbs of the city. We congratulated each other on what we saw as the huge stroke of luck by which we had arrived in Zaragoza at this moment in history.

In search of occupation to fill the rest of the day we were staggered to learn that the city was in the grip of a purity campaign, and no sooner had we appeared again in the street than we were encircled by young Leaguers of the Pure Lily who tried to pin flags on our shirts and to explain how best to keep ourselves unsullied by the world. A film company had been drawn into this and had issued a leaflet announcing a programme of films of a devotional character. Zaragoza had been spoken of by an American in San Sebastián as a place where they danced in the streets at night, but all this had come to an end, for part of the Leaguers' campaign included a drive to get people early to bed and early to rise.

In the old days many cafés in Zaragoza gave concerts based on such beloved folk music as the native *rondalla* of Aragon. This, the Pure Lily Leaguers criticised as not only worldly, but out of date. On the whole the Leaguers appeared to distrust art in all its forms, and only religious chanting in sessions held for this purpose was regarded as wholly acceptable. Nevertheless 'Hot Rhythm', having recently penetrated the cities of Spain, was tolerated if not approved, being seen merely as a passing fad and offering no threat to religious zeal.

The *paseo* still functioned, although the version permitted in Zaragoza kept the sexes apart, and phalanxes of frigid-faced girls marched up and down the promenade, a few carrying Leaguers' flags, and all stolidly indifferent to the usual compliments and solicitations of the soldiers of the town's garrison. We arrived on this scene at about 8 p.m., just as the girls marched off. With this, the *paseo* had disintegrated, leaving a residue of frustrated young males to be pestered by boys hired by a pharmaceutical firm as salesmen for a remedy for impotence.

Next morning came the news that, through some muddle

over the termination or not of the State of Alarm, the train for Madrid, originally scheduled for three in the afternoon, would not now be leaving until the morning of the next day. With this, quite suddenly, the mood in Zaragoza changed. Plans of all kinds were thrown into disarray, as illustrated by the case of the Granadina hotel whose sad and sallow rooms had been empty for weeks but were now suddenly filled in a single day. Chaos, we were to discover, was caused not only by the delay in the train's departure, but the arrival of large numbers of would-be travellers pouring in from the countryside and determined at all costs to escape the monotony of their existence during the Alarm.

Many had been travelling down the roads all through the night, and we were to discover that not only was the station waiting room crammed to the doors but luggage had been piled everywhere on the platforms themselves. We asked a railwayman how all these people and their possessions could be packed into a single train, and his reply was, 'Don't you worry, sir, we'll cram them in somehow. It's a big train as they go.'

It was a situation that left us with a free day. We decided to devote it to a health-giving walk out of town, to be followed by a swim in the river if we could manage to reach any part that was free from pollution.

To avoid having to traverse the rubbish dumps, we crossed the bridge before starting on our walk, finding ourselves in a matter of a few hundred yards in what might have been another continent. We had read somewhere of the beautiful wilderness across the river and it was immediately clear that this had been colonised by gypsies, of whom a hundred or so came into view. Spain, as we were soon to confirm, was probably the one country where this mysterious race had guarded its isolation. Here a considerable group had occupied a gently sloping bank down to the river.

The surroundings at this distance remained clean and fresh. The gypsies had rigged up a large tent of rags stitched together, and in casual openings in this, women in ankle-length dresses of garish colours appeared to be sharing domestic tasks. Small children dressed in an assortment of tatters ran out to waylay us. They were full of antics designed to draw our attention, laughing continually, but did not speak, and jumped up and down for joy when we handed out a few coins. Their mothers ignored us as if we were non-existent. We were amazed to find that these people had made some attempt to decorate their environment by sticking little clumps of coloured material in the surrounding grass. Soon a man rode up on a half-starved horse, with the bones sticking out of its hide. He took a number of plants out of his bag and passed them to the women. By now we had been asking ourselves how these people made a living, and the horseman, as we were later to learn, provided the answer in part. Much to the indignation of the medical profession, they made up and sold herbal remedies. They were also said to cast effective spells.

It was the best part of an hour's walk upstream from this point before the river and the landscape came into their own. At the beginning of our walk the water had been stained an acid yellow, with islands of flotsam spread over its surface. Now suddenly, and surprisingly, it had cleared with an abrupt widening of the river bed. This had become a hundred yards of sparkling white shingle, sharply defined by clean-cut perpendicular banks. Scattered through the acres of pebbles were shining pools connected by a curled thread representing the diminished volume of the river at the end of the dry season. The banks here were heavily wooded, and in places almost impassable through the tropical density of the undergrowth. This explosion of vegetation made frequent incursions into the river itself, and great clumps of grass, and sometimes even tough bushes, had thrust up through the stratum of polished stones.

The course of the river through this scenery was traced like an infinitely elongated oasis across the plains. In the middle distance an immense fir swayed rhythmically like a pendulum in reverse and cranes had taken possession of almost every branch. Finding a clear patch of shingle we decided to bathe, but having waded with difficulty over a patch of razor-edged stones, we found that the course of the river was now underneath an overhang of the opposite bank. Here, taken by surprise, we dropped suddenly into unfathomable depths and were instantly whirled away by the current. It required all our strength to save ourselves from drowning, and scrambling back eventually onto the bank we both agreed that it was the nearest to death we had ever been.

Next morning we received a final guarantee that the train for Madrid would leave at midday and that postponements were at an end. The station buildings, hotel, and their immediate surroundings were crammed with hopeful travellers and the many relatives who were there to see them off. Optimism was bolstered by the extra wagons that were to be added to the train to cope with an expected increase in the usual number of passengers. It was not to be armoured, as previously reported, to deal with the possibility of an attack by left-wing political fanatics. Instead it would carry an infantry platoon and in support of this assurance a dozen or so soldiers were to be seen drilling at the far end of one of the platforms.

A feeling that things were going well was increased by the news that porters had turned up for duty, and the bitter graffiti chalked on walls were in the course of being scrubbed off. An element of doubt still causing a little concern was that only a few first-class tickets had so far been distributed, leaving the vast majority of the remaining seats to be occupied by the first to reach them. The train pulled into the station on time, and while for a minute or two the Army and the police held back a surging multi-tude of non-ticket holders, we were included with the privileged dozen or so to be escorted to their seats. Within a matter of minutes a torrent of desperate humanity had broken through. Every seat in our compartment had gone. There were children round our feet and the corridor was jammed tight with the last to arrive.

A passenger seated with us had been on the telephone to Madrid minutes before catching the train. He was a left-winger and happy to be assured by whoever it was on the end of the line that the first shots of the coming revolu-tion had already been fired. Party members, however, he said, had been instructed by their leaders to abstain from action until they received orders to attack.

The conversation had taken a political turn when a diver-sion was created by a guard struggling his way through from the corridor.

'Tickets, please.'

'What for?' the passenger next to me shouted.

'No nonsense, please. Just show me your tickets.'

'We don't have any tickets. Tickets have been abolished.'

'Ah, so it's the revolution is it?'

'You're right. The revolution. Aren't you a member of the working class? Aren't you one of us, too? What are you going to do about it?'

'I propose to carry out my duty,' the guard said. 'According to regulations you will be charged double the normal fare.'

With this several of our fellow passengers grabbed the guard by the shoulder and hustled him out of the compartment.

Minutes later the train slowed to give us the opportunity to see an enthusiastic demonstration marching down a principal street of Catalayud behind a red banner bearing the words *Muerte Al Fascismo*. Suddenly the sound of shots rang out, and with the instant assumption that the train was under fire we were immediately engulfed in panic. The belief was that fire had been opened on the demonstrators from across the tracks, and this was evidently the case as windows on the far side of the corridor were shattered by bullets. The corridor was submerged with shrieking panic-stricken passengers, a number of whom had already been swept off their feet. By the time the train jerked forward and began to accelerate out of range of what was generally taken to be sniper fire, the log jam of humanity struggling in the corridor was finally released, leaving an unmistakable whiff of urine in the air.

A few miles further on more distant shots were heard. Soldiers of our escort appeared at each end of the carriage to poke their guns through the windows and fire at some target invisible to us, and with this panic returned. By this time our compartment held roughly double the number of passengers stipulated by the notice, and it was inevitable that refugees who had been unable to secure a seat should squat on the floor, forced sometimes to wedge themselves between the legs of those who travelled in greater comfort. Children wailed, and a woman dabbed at a sore place on her arm with the hem of her skirt. Listening to the sound of rifle fire we wondered who was firing at whom, and why. Were the travellers on this train assumed by those who took aim from the suburbs of Catalayud to be the supporters of the revolution, or the reverse, or the enemies of the proletariat? That was something we would never know.

CHAPTER 5

THE SUBURBS OF Madrid, sprawling in all directions, seemed remarkably deserted, although as was soon to be evident, much of their population were taking cover. The train rattled into the main station of Mediodía Madrid, a vast terminus where at first no one was to be seen, and once again there was good reason for this emptiness. As soon as the train came to a standstill an undisciplined scramble for the platform took place and Eugene and I dropped our luggage through the window and clambered down. Once free of the train, indecision took over. Crashing fusillades at close quarters seemed to be coming from the direction of the station outbuildings, and at intervals of a few seconds a major explosion echoed with shattering reverberations under the enormously wide glass roof of the station, and glass came crashing down.

The passengers, laden with bundles, were running along the platform, and a small crowd had gathered at the exit although no one passed through the doors. No screams were to be heard in this vast, apprehensive near-silence. A cluster of small holes had suddenly appeared in the nearby glass partition, all fringed with a frosty radiance of cracks.

Down at the end of the platform, by the various waiting rooms and offices, our fellow passengers had gathered in a little frightened herd, some squeezing themselves into angles of the wall. It is impossible to conceive of a less satisfactory place in which to take cover than a large railway station. There seemed to be glass everywhere, and there was not a single nook, corner or cranny where one could be certain not to be hit by a bullet. That is to say with the possible exception of the lavatories, but to reach these asylums meant negotiating the particularly exposed intervening fifty yards.

The buffet was actually open and someone suggested this as a potential fastness. But here again the walls were only about nine feet high. After that more glass. It would have been the easiest thing in the world to have lobbed a grenade in through the window and blown the place to smithereens. At this point one of the station personnel rushed in to warn us that something like a pitched battle between revolutionaries and infantrymen was being fought in a nearby courtyard, and every few seconds we could hear the crash of a grenade.

Nevertheless, being both hungry and thirsty, we decided to risk the buffet, and going in found the man who ran the place still at the counter, although clearly shaking in his shoes.

'Any coffee?' I asked.

'No coffee.' He shook his head.

'Wine, then?'

'No wine.'

'Anyway, I see you've got some orangeade there.'

'Help yourself,' the man said.

We drank the orangeade and put down a ten-peseta note. He shook his head and we went out. From where we stood among the broken glass we got a glimpse out into the street. It was a small, square patch of sunshine framed in the doorway where the ticket collector usually stands. This brilliant little scene was bisected by a gently sloping wall behind which occasionally passed the heads and shoulders of citizens of Madrid who were walking with their hands held aloft.

From time to time an exceptionally heavy volley would ring out and any of the moving busts in sight would be suddenly withdrawn from the field of vision, although whether the owner had been struck down, or was adopting a prone position out of prudence, it was impossible to say. Immediately adjacent to the doorway on the station wall an alluring travel poster bore the inscription in English 'Spain Attracts and Holds You. Under the Blue Skies of Spain Cares are Forgotten.'

It seemed to us that the armed forces occupying the station were quite inadequate to hold off a really determined onslaught by the revolutionaries occupying some of the outer buildings. Drawn up in front of us in a straggling double rank was a squad of some twenty soldiers. They seemed fully to share our fears over the lack of cover and the open windows, and kept glancing nervously upwards in the hope of avoiding the continuing showers of glass. They were conscripts ranging in age from eighteen to twenty-one and seemed to be extremely nervous. The sudden shriek of an engine whistle produced a moment of demoralisation in the troops and they clutched their rifles in such a desperate fashion that we feared accidental discharges. A foreign journalist who had come in on our train went up to the officer.

'Do you think it's worth trying to get across the street?'

'Wait until it quietens down a bit. You might make a run for it.'

'Is it necessary to keep my hands up?'

'Unless you're tired of life. If you get caught in a squall, drop down just where you are and don't be in a hurry to get up.'

At the end of a couple of hours or so the shots became more infrequent. We listened to the occasional distant volleys, but the zone of the fighting seemed to be moving away from the station. There was a small hotel directly opposite the station entrance and we hoped to be able to cross the road and find a room for the night. At that moment several of the people from our train demonstrated how this was to be done.

Passing out through the station doors they raised their hands and walked cautiously to the kerb's edge. Here the group came to a standstill while each member looked in both directions before, hands still raised, taking the first cautious step into the road. At that moment two hand grenades exploded somewhere in the vicinity and to our intense surprise these people dropped to the ground and began to cross the road on their hands and knees. Their action set the example for more refugees from the station. We, too, decided to make the crossing. Raising our hands, we stepped down from the kerb and began to walk slowly and with a certain dignity, we hoped, among the crawlers, making for the small hotel. We had reached the middle of the road when a cavalry squadron swept into sight, reined in their horses and opened fire. With that, we too dropped to the ground and began crawling with the rest. The horsemen charged through, leaving one of those who had risked the road-crossing – as we were later to learn – shot dead.

The owner of the small hotel had been deserted by his staff and was moving out, he told us, as soon as he could do so. He was sure that the Mediodía area would be the centre of the battle for the city, expected to be unleashed, he said, that evening. This, he considered, would result in a victory for the Reds, a prospect for which he had little relish. 'They take life too seriously,' he said. 'I'm in business to enjoy myself and have a little fun. I'll wait until things settle down. By that time nobody will have any money and I'll be able to pick up a cabaret for nothing and have a good time again.' He could give us a room for that night, he said. After that he might close down until people stopped shooting each other. Most hotels were closed for the emergency, he explained, but he gave us the address of a working man's boarding house on the northern side of the town. 'You have to look after yourself,' he said, 'but it's cheap. Ask for a top-floor room. They're the cheapest, and not much bigger than a kennel. But let's suppose they start a battle in the street, you could always get out on the roof. You'd have a mile of roofs to play hide-and-seek on. The boss is called Felipe. Tell him Salvador sent you. It's a long walk, maybe two miles, but keep your hands up all the way. Stick to the Avenidas. In the side streets you're likely to get yourselves shot as Reds.'

'So the reactionaries are still hanging on,' I said.

'They're at their last gasp,' Salvador assured us. 'Tomorrow the big offensive begins and they'll finish them off. All you have to do is stay alive until then.'

We stood at the door and watched people streaming past, dodging in and out of shop doorways and doing their best to keep under cover. Nine shops out of ten were closed and most people were out trying to buy food. They all still walked with their hands held up, and there was something about this city that reminded me of a weird and complicated child's toy. Not only were people reaching for the sky, but under the stress of fear they seemed to move in a jerky, mechanical fashion. Although we were surrounded by tall buildings that suppressed the sounds of battle, we could still hear the crack of hand grenades exploding in the backstreets, and the occasional splutter of a machine-gun.

CHAPTER 6

WE FOUND FELIPE at his desk in the basement of his tall, grey, narrow hotel, and decided that Salvador had by no means exaggerated his description of it as being working-class. It contained a large number of clean, severely-furnished rooms which were available at the equivalent of roughly one shilling and six pence per person a night. Notices admonished guests to observe rigid moral standards. Anyone, said a large placard, failing to observe the rules of education and punctilious manners would be expelled instantly, whatever the hour of day or night. 'There is no restaurant,' Felipe said, 'but you may bring down your tray for morning coffee, midday and evening meals, and then return with it to your room.' A mole twitched continually on his left cheek as he spoke, and his expression in between sentences was victimised by an unfocused smile.

'Salvador spoke about the roof terrace,' I said.

'He's right,' Felipe agreed. 'Your room will be on the top floor. It will be easy for you to reach the roof, but equally easy for someone you may not wish to see to enter your room. Remember that we have a secret police.'

What we hadn't realised at first was that Felipe's hotel was just inside the frontier of the working-class district of

Atocha. We took a short exploratory walk, although in the wrong direction. By turning left we should have reached in about five minutes an area of palm-shaded avenues and small, respectable parks. As it was we turned right into what remained of the unimproved Madrid. At this particular moment it had become one of the principal foci of the class struggle, and a few hundred yards across the Atocha frontier trams, although empty of passengers, carried four soldiers on the front platform and four more at the rear.

Fear held Atocha in its grip. There was an occasional ping of a sniper's rifle followed by a wild fusillade as the police let go at suspicious objects. The newly-created Assault Guards had been brought in to take on the revolutionaries. Most of them were in their early twenties, and I had read in a newspaper that many had been chosen not for their military bearing but their good looks. Here under the sniper fire in Atocha they seemed to be terror-stricken, blazing away with their German sub-machine-guns at windows and rooftops. One who had been wounded in the arm was crying like a child.

Setting out from the hotel, we were anxious not to surrender to an overdramatisation of the events, covering the first few hundred yards as if enjoying a leisurely morning stroll. We were converted by the sight of a well-dressed citizen lying in the gutter with something like red jelly spread over his chest at the opening of his shirt. Turning a corner moments later, we faced a machine-gun pointing vaguely at our stomachs and were halted by the threatening yell of the gunner. With that we came into line with the Madrileños, our hands went up, and we turned back.

We stopped for a drink at the Bar Atocha. I could not

get over my amazement that whatever the danger and drama out in the streets, places like this not only stayed open but attracted business. To lessen the possibility of being robbed by death of his clientele the owner had cut off the main part of his café with a barricade of chairs and tables. There was a line of bullet holes across the window from one end of the café to the other. Even the bar itself was chipped and splintered by ricocheting bullets and a blood splash on the floor had not been wholly scrubbed out.

The owner was a Cuban from Havana who spoke American English which he kept trim, he said, by a daily visit to a cinema specialising in American films. This was his sixth revolution, but his first experience of the Spanish version, where, he explained with approval, they made a point of doing their best not to shoot a man in the cobblers. 'The smart thing they do here when a man goes looking for a battle is to have a broad carry the gun. The one thing you have to hand to these guys is they never search the women.'

The day before had been a bad one. As he had left the café to go home he had been arrested and hauled off to the police station where they pushed him around a bit but then let him go.

'What about today?' I asked him. 'What's the programme for the day?'

'Oh, I guess it's safe enough in the morning,' he said. 'Put it this way, people need a break to do their shopping.'

'How about the afternoon?'

'Well, I guess that's different. Maybe you heard. The Red Army has to come out some time before tonight.'

'And will it?'

'Christ only knows. Maybe it will, maybe it won't. The

guys at the top have to get together and stop the arguments. All depends on what comes through from Barcelona and the North.'

'So what's happening up there?'

'They declared a separate state, but it's supposed to have fizzled out already. News is that Asturias has gone Red. General López Ochoa was sent up there but they say the Reds derailed the train and cut his head off.'

'What about the Reds in this city? Are they well armed?'

'The usual thing. Machine-guns and hand grenades. We shan't know much about it until later in the day. Right now they're knocking out police stations and barracks. If they go down, the churches will go up.'

'Why should that be?' Eugene asked.

'Because these guys hate the work of the Almighty Lord.'

'That's bad,' Eugene told him. 'But why?'

'Because that's the way they are.'

'From what you say we ought to be moving on and looking for a quieter place.'

'No hurry, it's not much past ten now. You've got until at least two before the trouble starts. That's when I'm shutting up. Hop into the nearest shop if anything starts. You don't have to worry about the Assault Guards so much, unless they get really sore. It's the untrained soldiers who can't shoot straight that bother me. If you're caught in some bad shooting don't try to run for it. Just lie down in the street wherever you happen to be, and wait till it stops. Better if you can eat in a place where the waiter puts on a uniform, and when you need to shop choose one with an elevator. Best shopping as you probably know is round the Mediodía Station. You can always pop in and study the timetables if the shooting starts.'

And this, without warning, it did, and too late the shop-keepers struggled to get their shutters down as bullets demolished their windows and glass showered on the pavements. Machine-guns stamped an orderly pattern across the anarchic clamour of pistol and rifle reports. People were collapsing as they ran, doubling up and sprawling in the roadway, having fainted, stopped a bullet or collapsed from sheer terror. With tyres squealing a car lurched out of a side street. The inside back wheel bumped heavily on the kerb, and we sensed rather than saw that a machine-gun was being fired from it. An elderly man running towards us stopped suddenly, as if he had forgotten something, before turning to bolt into a shop doorway where he fell on his knees. Somehow we were able to extricate ourselves and reach the shelter of the hotel. The hubbub spreading up the side streets from the Puerta del Sol was close on our heels.

Back at the hotel we found the residents grouped on the stairs. This, through long experience, was deemed to be the safest place in such an emergency. We pushed past them and went up to our top room on the corner. From there we had an unobstructed view in three directions. At this height the racket was even more appalling; the individual reports produced by a variety of firearms amalgamated in a vast blur of sound. Assault Guards were advancing up the side streets, hugging the walls and exchanging fire with unseen adversaries on the roofs. Directly below on the opposite side of the road was a pork butcher's shop whose owner had been too late to get the shutters up. While we looked on from our balcony the windows collapsed under a machine-gun volley. We were later to discover it had inflicted posthumous lesions on the porkers still suspended on their hooks.

Once or twice a distant scream asserted itself above the clamour. In a brief interlude of silence we heard the tapping of a blind beggar's stick in the street below. He was lurching wildly and appeared to be hit. Two workers rushed out and took him by the arms, disappearing round one corner as an Assault Guard came into sight round the other. He pointed his rifle at our window. We slammed the shutters and stood back against the wall. No shot was fired, and as soon as it seemed safe to change our position we got out of the room and went downstairs.

A great assortment of ordinary people caught up in the street battle had taken refuge in the hotel. Left-wing strikers from the factories who had thrown their guns away when things got bad and made a dash for the nearest open door mixed with peasants who had come up, as they frankly admitted, to see the fun. The restaurant had opened at the usual evening hour but served nothing but coffee, and a doctor attended to the wounds of a guest stretched out on a table, whose screams, since no anaesthetics were available, added to the pandemonium.

Two communists introduced themselves politely and sat down at our table. They announced their political views with the pride with which in medieval days a man might have claimed membership of some knightly order. 'Good evening, I am Manuel Maltés. This is my friend, Esteban Iriarte.' Manuel was a mountainous Andalusian, a lawyer who had renounced collar, tie and razor as a tribute to his political views. Esteban, a cadaverous-faced Madrileño with melancholy eyes, a nostalgic expression and a gentle voice, appeared to be the intellectual disciple of the first.

The memory of that great propagandist of the English Bible, George Borrow, was still green in Spain. At this time I was the brief possessor of a beard, and the word had gone round among our Spanish acquaintances that we were engaged in the sale of bibles. These two militant atheists had apparently thought that it would be amusing to draw us into taking up the cudgels for Christ. With this misapprehension out of the way, Manuel recited poetry of the elemental kind, talking of such fundamental things as birth, life and the earth. Esteban hung on his words with the tears rolling down his face.

The varying thicknesses of wall separating us from the street had partially blanketed out the sounds of the battle. Only the constant crash of grenades exploding close to the hotel shattered the moments of silence, jarred the crockery and set the pans jangling in the kitchen. In the intervals a loudspeaker somewhere in the street brayed out messages of comfort and reassurance. 'We are happy to be able to announce to our listeners that complete tranquillity has been restored throughout Spain.'

'Turn it off,' yelled a voice.

'No, leave it alone,' said another, 'it won't be long before our fellows take over the station.'

Among the more disturbing reports was one saying that the communists would that night use a plane to bomb the Gobernación – the Ministry of the Interior – which was located in an immense complex of buildings two streets away. The difficulty with this project, according to a comrade who had served in the Air Force, was that the lack of practice at such a nocturnal assault would expose a large part of the area to considerable risk.

Another factor bothering our new acquaintances was that a resident might be tempted to strike a blow for Socialism by sniping from the hotel, thus producing police reprisals of a vigorous and undiscriminating kind. While this was under discussion a man in his working clothes came in and sat down at the next table. He had been wounded in the neck, which was wrapped with a blood-soaked scarf. A basin of soup was produced in his honour, and this he drank with some difficulty and much coughing. The soup finished, he called over a woman and emptied two pocketfuls of bullets into her lap. This was done without attempt at concealment.

A few minutes later there was a loud report seeming to come from the direction of the skylight, which was repeated at intervals. This attracted the notice of two Assault Guards outside in a car. They shone a searchlight at the door but, possibly believing themselves to be outnumbered, drove off.

Next morning we got up and went down to the Puerta del Sol for breakfast. It was served, revolution or not, with the speed and good humour of any normal day. Everywhere the walls were flecked with bullet marks. Every shop window in sight had been punctured or devastated by direct hits or flying fragments. The Gobernación remained inviolate. It was surrounded by a large force of Assault Guards brought there in vehicles like old-fashioned brakes, with open sides and therefore offering no protection for the guards perched in rows on unprotected benches. Three trams had been derailed, but the revolutionaries had now been replaced by sightseers, and a group of Guards were no more than entertained by a lunatic who threatened them with a child's toy gun.

CHAPTER 7

AT DAWN THE next day, all was quiet. Soon after daybreak we were called to the window by the sounds of jingling harnesses and plopping hooves. A squad of steel-helmeted cavalry was defiling down the street towards the centre of town. I decided that the Spanish army was yet another military machine that hoped to acquire martial virtue by moulding itself externally on the pattern of the Reichswehr. There was even something Germanic about the shrieked word of command.

We got up and again went down to the Puerta del Sol for breakfast. Much as on the previous day, the morning vitality of Madrid had been in no way damaged by the night alarms. There were new bullet marks on the walls. Every other shop window had been punctured by direct hits or devastated by flying fragments. The Gobernación remained inviolate and was still surrounded by a large force of Assault Guards.

Outside the Gobernación a queue had been formed to buy *El Debate*, the clerical newspaper, which, being unpopular among the working population, was being sold under police protection. We stood in the queue until the supply was exhausted, and then wandered away.

In the Calle Alcalá an ordinary newspaper-seller was

doing a brisk trade with the *ABC*. This was a notable and somewhat reactionary daily. Just as we came up he stuffed the remaining copies under his coat and walked away quickly. We went after him and offered him ten times the usual price for a copy. He rejected our offer, telling us that he had just been warned on pain of death to stop selling.

In the main thoroughfares round the Puerta del Sol, well-dressed youths had brought out a municipal dust-van and were clearing up the rubbish. They were attacking the work with a great show of animal spirit, taking a special delight in showering the refuse over each other's neatly creased trousers and scintillating shoes. The yells of joy when one of them tripped on the edge of the van and fell into the muck nearly started an alarm.

More trams were running and the confusion had correspondingly increased. Casting an eye round the Puerta del Sol it was not uncommon to see two or three stranded trams which had somehow or other got on to the wrong line or had been derailed. These would be surrounded by a perplexed group of soldiers and a large crowd of discreetly jeering citizens. This factor, combined with the evidence of the bullet-shattered glass and woodwork, suggested that tram riding had become more a matter of high adventure than convenience.

In the cafés, stories were circulating of the night's slaughters. Apart from café-visiting there was very little we dared do. It was unsafe to get out of sight of the Puerta del Sol. Above all we were anxious not to get cut off from our retreat by a machine-gun battle. So most of our time in those early days in Madrid was spent in cafés.

The first place we visited was of the variety where you paid nine pence for a cup of coffee; the charge being based on three pence for materials and sixpenny worth of atmosphere. It was frequented by substantial business-men, one of whom was describing to his cronies at the neighbouring table adversities he had suffered the night before. He was impressed by the bitter irony of having been hounded through the streets by the police who were paid to protect his interests.

He described his experience in a billiard room over a fashionable café when the firing had started, and the police (so he said, although it sounded improbable) had mistaken the tapping of cues for some sort of muffled firearm. Anyway, to promote a submissive attitude they had thrown a hand grenade through a window and then charged in. The businessmen, probably gouty, undoubt-edly short-winded, had been driven down the stairs and out into the street, while the police fired pot-shots at them from the café windows. The narrator had then made for home, a journey which, having been made for the greater part of the distance on his hands and knees, had taken him several hours to complete.

When we finally managed to buy a paper, it made small reference to recent events. The death was reported of a woman who had been shot through the heart when she had opened her bedroom window to see what was going on. Names were published of a few civilians who had been mown down in the street. Most of the space was devoted to commendations of the soldiers and police, and accounts of how by their unflagging bravery, devotion and loyalty in the hour of national need, normality was now restored.

Having no faith in the propagandist conception of normality, we began to edge, early in the afternoon, in the direction of the hotel. It was 3.30 p.m. The Puerta del Sol was as thickly populated as ever, but today a neurotic jumpiness was noticeable in the crowd. As usual we stopped at the Levante for a drink, finding that so far it had come off comparatively unscathed. It was a splendid place in which to relax and we hoped that the proprietor of this excellent café had managed to remain on good terms with the police.

We had been looking forward to another hour's liberty before taking cover for the night, but no sooner had we given our order than we noted that the Puerta del Sol was already emptying. Two men ran past. We decided to bank on intuition and got up to go. Our uneasiness seemed contagious. Almost as one man the patrons of the Levante drained their glasses. With a perfectly synchronised scuffle, chairs were pushed back. A dozen voices bellowed for the bill and at least as many, remaining silent, decided to settle up on a more propitious occasion.

Just as we pushed through the doors the expected shot rang out: that now unpleasantly familiar sound, the harbinger of panic at whose signal the general stampede would commence. With the faultless unanimity of a well-ordered puppet show, all hands went up. The Assault Guards clenched their teeth and raised their rifles. In ten seconds the Puerta del Sol was a desert. The inevitable diminutive soldier with the large automatic herded us into a bar on the street corner. The bar was open on two sides. It would have taken about ten minutes to get the complicated shutters down. The barman, deciding that even to make the attempt would be unprofitable, contented himself by whisking down out of harm's way the more expensive bottles of drink.

Almost as soon as we got back to the hotel there was a rapping on the door. Two detectives stood outside. Keeping their right hands significantly in their pockets,

they used the left to uncover, with a gesture last seen in
Wild West movies, their stars of authority. With many
apologies they examined our passports, searched our
baggage and looked under the bed for hidden ammunition.
What was worrying them was the presence in a cheap
working-class hotel of two men who carried masculine
fashion to the extent of a collar and tie. We assured them
we represented the English equivalent of their own pro-
letarians, but that owing to the successes in our country
of the capitalist social order our standard of living had been
raised. Consequently we were in a position to ape the fashions of our betters. They were impressed, and wished that
they could honestly say the same about Spain. But as we
could see for ourselves there existed at the moment a regret-
table lack of unanimity of opinion regarding the benefits
conferred by capitalism.

With nightfall, a searchlight that had been mounted on
the highest building in Madrid – the Capitol Cinema –
came into play. It swept the roofs with a double shaft of
light that looked almost solid in the dark sky. In view of
the non-appearance on the streets of any organised socialist
forces, the Government had decided to declare war on the
snipers.

Seen from a suitable eminence, the most essential
characteristic of Madrid is the flatness of its roofs. Layer
upon layer of roofs rise one behind the other, their conti-
nuity broken by innumerable attic windows and odd addi-
tional storeys; creepers, which in season bear red and
purple flowers, twine about them. The sea of tiles, toned
by the sun and mellowed by grime to a charming compromise between black and yellow, with faded touches of gold,
is an altogether Spanish and most attractive sight. This
characteristic roof is known as the *azotea*. It has played a

considerable part in determining the character of warfare on Spanish soil.

The *azotea* is the answer to a sniper's dream. The facilities it offers for well-sustained guerrilla warfare coupled with centuries of practice have produced a special technique of attack. It was estimated, according to one of the papers, that ten thousand snipers were operating from the *azoteas* during the first few nights of the revolt. Granted that in the majority of cases these snipers were boys armed with cheap Belgian revolvers, the bullets of which were almost harmless by the time they reached the street, they still constituted a nightmare for the military authorities.

The average sniper's method of procedure involved no great risk. All that was necessary was to clamber to the roof of the house where he lived or lodged, cross over to someone else's roof, select a nicely-sheltered position overlooking the street where he could see without being seen, and then empty his revolver at the first Assault Guard in sight. After that he could retire while things simmered down. In the days of Napoleon it took the demolition of half the city to clear out ten thousand of these partisans. But nowadays conditions had changed. The police gave orders for all access to the *azoteas* or terraces to be closed. The searchlight bathed the roofs of the city in a blueish white glare in imitation of daylight. The Guards and the soldiers followed its beam with their rifles. In the morning they went round collecting the bodies of those who had still believed in the triumph of the revolution.

CHAPTER 8

ON FRIDAY, OCTOBER 12, what had been described in the press as the Battle of Madrid faltered to an end. There was no official statement about the end of hostilities in this small local war, but it was evident that the snipers had left the rooftops, the shopkeepers had removed their window shutters, and most of the Assault Guards were back in their barracks. We saw no displays of relief in what might have been described as a stunned calm following the battle in this extraordinary city. Working-class families in the under-privileged areas of Atocha and Tetuan tasted once more the pleasures of the streets. The sellers of obscene books had set up their stalls again and drew small crowds, slyly turning over the much fingered leaves, although rarely buying.

Vendors of blinded singing birds had set out their three-inch high cages on the pavements, and 'beggars' – side-shows of human beings with grotesquely distorted heads, bodies or limbs – were put on display in the dark, inner slum courtyards, viewers being supplied with torches for a small payment. By ten in the morning it was estimated that little short of a thousand of the more affluent citizens were once again taking coffee in the top cafés, while symbolically prostrate rows of boot-blacks worked on their shoes.

We spent the afternoon drifting from café to café with our Spanish friends Manuel and Estebán, both of whom were expecting to be arrested and were anxious, on what would probably be their last day of liberty, to savour its joys (the highest expression of which was café visiting) to the very full.

Next morning Estebán disappeared. Manuel decided to leave while the going was good. Later in the day he came to say goodbye to us. There was a great deal of shaking of hands and slapping of shoulders. During the few days we had known Manuel we had become greatly attached to him. He was an affectionate and enthusiastic fellow; a Utopian and a visionary, full of great thoughts and charming fallacies – but like so many of his kind threatened by a premature doom. We later learned that he had been arrested immediately after leaving us.

It had been agreed between us that Eugene would be free to go his own way if he wanted to get more closely involved in the present crisis. A contingent of what by this time had come to be described as the Red Army was moving down on the capital from the North, and was at that moment in the vicinity of Camillas, a small town some fifteen miles to the city's south. Here it was in the process of enlisting other militant groups in the neighbourhood before what was hoped to be the final attack on Madrid. This was expected to be launched in less than a week's time. Eugene, of course, was wildly enthusiastic about the possibility of joining this group, and had received the warmest possible encouragement from Manuel and his friends. His only remaining problem was how to get to Camillas. The news was that the many wrecked vehicles until recently blocking the road had been cleared, and that farm-carts were able to get through. Eugene had been assured that we could reach this small town in a day. His further argument was that even should it be impossible to get a lift, we had far exceeded a hike of this length on a single good morning in our walk earlier in the month.

It was settled that I would go with him as far as Camillas, but I made it quite clear that I had no intention of joining in the final attack on the capital itself – nor in any other military adventure undertaken by the so called Red Army. We set out next morning shortly after dawn and it very soon became clear that this was a journey by no means likely to compare in any respect with the uncomplicated stroll to Zaragoza.

There was nothing to eat in any of the cafés in Madrid, so we made for the Levante for a drink of their own creation designed to camouflage the staleness of the accompanying biscuit. A few more trams had appeared and we took one on which a line of evenly spaced bullet holes remained along a bench on which passengers would once have been seated. The latest plague was an invasion by starving, semi-wild dogs, and one had just been destroyed by a guard at the entrance to the Cuatro Caminos station. Here we had hoped for seats on a train to take us at least halfway on our journey to Camillas. We were advised by the stationmaster to return next day when it was hoped that an armed guard would be found to accompany us on the journey. We asked him who would provide the guard – the Gobernación, or the People's Militia – and he replied that he hadn't the faintest idea. Then, by the greatest of good luck, he remembered that a hearse would be calling to leave a coffin at the station, and the driver, when it arrived, was happy to give us a lift for a few miles on our way.

Thereafter we were free of the city and on the open road lined with small villages in the process of becoming suburbs. They seemed to us to have retained a certain oriental flavour with the small windows of their houses deeply set in white-washed walls and their robust chimneys – also whitewashed – projecting from flat roofs. To me it looked like Agadir, in South Morocco – particularly where goats were to be seen tethered on a roof. For me this was Islam.

These people, said our driver, were the owners of a single cow, or even more often a single goat. There was an old law – called by the Spanish a *fuera* (meaning privilege) – by which the peasantry in some village communes were allowed to buy a quarter of a square mile of land from its feudal owner for an exceedingly low price. To qualify for this the peasant had to throw a lead ball, weighing ten kilograms, five metres.

Travelling wizards visited these villages to deal with a variety of sicknesses, most reported as having a sexual origin. Other specialist healers paid regular calls to treat sore feet, eye troubles, and depression in general, and sometimes to save time and expenses the various healers travelled together in bands. Although primitive – as they admitted even to themselves – these communities lived, on the whole, satisfactory lives. All their recent problems were blamed on the present right-wing government which had allowed speculators to double prices, thus compelling these simple country folk to learn what communism was all about. Political agents from Camillas appeared on the scene to tell them that their first step was to fly the red flag on their roofs. This they did and the next day the Assault Guards arrived in an armoured car and shot the roof off wherever a red flag was to be seen.

We arrived in Camillas in the early afternoon. What was

remarkable about this small town was that back at the end of the nineteenth century the leading citizen was a villain who carried out a massive fraud by which most of its inhabitants were ruined. After this he escaped to Holland where he started a religious sect known as The Unseen Power. This was to become the most influential of many such movements in the Low Countries. Returning to Camillas some years later, he put things right with all his victims and left a memory of his presence in the shape of a nativity play. This, despite the disapproval of the Holy Church, continued to attract immense local audiences, and even foreign pilgrims, until its final suppression.

Our arrival coincided with the day when the long-awaited advance of the 'Red Army' was to take place. The critics were already murmuring that this had been too long delayed. A revolutionary citizens' army, bolstered so strongly as it had been by enthusiasm and ideals, might only four days earlier have routed an uninspired opposition. The loss of the four days had given the Government the time it needed to ready itself for action, but nevertheless, Camillas with its flower bombardments, parading volunteers, the captured cannon, and the brass band still managed to be in good heart.

There was a bust of Lenin, brushed over with aluminium paint, on the café table and a small red flag was given away free with a cup of coffee. The scene was one of nervous good humour. Four smallish teenage girls in soldiers' uniforms were surrounded by admirers, and we arrived at the moment when they had decided to shear a few inches off the tunics' sleeves to smarten them up. A middle-aged captain with a greying walrus moustache was in command here, and I waited my turn to ask him a question. 'How far away are the Fascists at the moment?'

'No way of knowing,' he said. 'We've got them on the run. Getting out while they can. That's if we let them. Are you a volunteer?'

'No, my friend is,' I told him.

'They told me about him. English, isn't he?'

'That's right.'

'Well, we'll be going after them any minute now. You ought to come along with us anyway. Be quite an experience.'

'Thanks. Perhaps I will,' I said.

The moment had come. I decided to tackle Eugene on his volunteer obsession, and I took him aside. 'I gave your father a promise to look after you,' I said, 'and that naturally included bringing you back alive.'

He laughed. 'That's understood,' he said. 'You're not going to let him down.'

'What you don't seem to be able to see is that the Red Army we've been hearing so much about is a figment of the imagination. They were supposed to have entered Madrid by today. Where are they?'

'I've just listened to the six o'clock news,' he said. 'They were reported to have occupied Tetuan this morning.'

'I listened to the eight o'clock news,' I told him. 'Nothing was said about it. The locals don't take these stories seriously any more. What they *do* believe is that a thousand of the new Assault Guards took over the central area of the city yesterday.'

'We shall have to wait and see,' Eugene said. 'In the meantime, have they told you about Casas Viejas?'

'No,' I said. 'What about it?'

'It's a village in the hills five or six miles from here. It was occupied a week or two ago by the Liberation Army.

We could go and see it for ourselves if you like. The road is open. Why don't we do that?'

'I'll do a deal with you,' I told him. 'Your father provided all the necessary funds for this trip, the objective so far as he was concerned being the pilgrimage to Seville. I can't see myself going back to break the news to him that you've joined a revolutionary army. I'll go to Casas Viejas with you and talk to the Liberation Army people, but after that we must either go on to Seville, or I personally shall feel obliged to turn round and go home.'

'What happens about the tickets and the money?'

'I'll have to think about that. It's his money. It would be a question of ringing him up and finding out what he wants done. You have to realise that the responsibility is mine.'

'So there's nothing for it really?'

'No, not really.'

'But you wouldn't object to going over to Casas Viejas?'

'No, why should I? It should be an interesting experience.'

I had read somewhere that twenty-odd villages scattered throughout Spain bore this name. It meant simply that they were old. Nothing was said about starving to death. It was a place name likely to be found among the swamps of a river delta, or the barren lower slopes of a mountain range, or in a borderland area of a province subject to invasion by starving soldiers from across the frontier.

The café-owner's younger brother, who was an enthusiastic Red, was happy to run us over there in his veteran Seat through a landscape turning into a wilderness within a mile of the village. A few twisted oaks had been able to root themselves among the rocks, but were shortly to be smothered by a dense growth of spiny bushes. I asked the driver what was the attraction of the place. Why on earth did people go there? 'The mountains,' he explained. 'The Guadarramas. Tourists come here for the view. We bottle up the water from the river down there and sell it for the nerves.'

Casas Viejas was round the next corner and proved to be just as expected. Order of a kind has to exist in these old places by the simple fact that everything worth having is kept, and nothing's thrown away. There is no rubbish. This could have been a village scene put together for an exhibition and tidied up every morning before the show opened. It was empty and silent, with its people housed in hutments with minute, square windows built as high as they could be from the ground, and a massive door sagging on its hinges. A notice stuck to a shed in the tiny square said, 'Viva España Soviética.' An old man, with a woman at his back, was at a door. The man bowed. 'There's no one here to talk to you but us people,' he said.

'Which direction did they take?' the driver asked. 'The People's Army, I mean.'

The man straightened up to point ahead. 'They went up that road,' he said, 'and then the next turning to the left just before you get to the top of the hill.'

'There should have been a fair number of them,' I told him. 'People's Army men with red flashes on their tunics.'

'That's right,' he said, 'red flashes as you say. I don't know one army from another, but I noticed the flashes. I'm only on holiday up here for a couple of days. Mind you, you couldn't get an army up that road. This wasn't an army. It was just a few soldiers.'

'Give me a rough idea how many. Fifty? A hundred?'

'Well, say fifty. Maybe less. This wasn't an army of any

kind. Red or otherwise. You could say there was a half-company of soldiers at most. Some didn't even have guns. If the Guards go after them they won't stand a chance.'

'Hold on a moment,' I said. 'What Guards are you talking about?'

'The Assault Guards from Madrid.'

'What, here?'

'There's a few of them down past the village. They came in when I was down there and pulled in off the road behind the Egg-Cup Hill.'

'But what are they doing there?' I asked him.

'Nothing.' He smiled as if at his inner thoughts. 'Just waiting's my guess.'

'They're waiting,' Eugene said, 'to take our friends in the rear.'

By the greatest possible luck the driver who'd given us the lift was still there and quite happy to take us to the junction with the Madrid road. 'I'm a widower,' he said, 'with nothing to do with my time. I'll have to leave you to look after yourselves at the turning to Madrid. If the Guards catch me with you they'll blow my van apart. Used to be a football ground up there once, but the people lost interest and it's all thorn bushes now. The Guards go up in their four-wheel drives but you'd never get anywhere in an old wreck like this. Lucky you came after they've just done the autumn cut-back of the jungle, otherwise you'd never even get through.'

It was three or four hundred yards to the turn-off but when we were halfway there we were already breathing in the sharp odour of the sap still oozing from cut stems. The opening into what was left of the bushes would have taken two cars but it soon narrowed to a bottle-neck and Eugene, who suffered from hay-fever, began to sneeze. Rodrigo, our driver, was proud of the barbarity of the past. 'Used to be a prison camp up here,' he said. 'That was before my time. Rapists were given six months in an open camp. The way they made them work they couldn't breathe properly. Most of them died of lung trouble before they could finish their sentence.'

The van, picking its way in low gear round the stumps, overheated, lost power, and finally we stopped. Rodrigo lifted the bonnet and let it drop. He switched off the engine and looked at his watch. There was a moment of silence, then we heard the roar of a powerful car climbing the hill, with no possible doubt that the Assault Guards were on our track. 'Better make a run for it,' Rodrigo said. 'I'll stay with the car.'

For a moment at least, the Assault Guards would be held up by Rodrigo's van, before they butted it aside with their powerful vehicle. We decided to run for it, cutting across country as far as we could before making a cautious return to the road. We were ready with a story that we were collecting specimens for a natural history magazine and I had warned Eugene to throw his party card away, which he refused to do.

Clambering down an easy slope where the thorn bushes were less of a thicket, we were suddenly alarmed by a burst of gunfire behind us and overtaken by panic we tried to tear our way through. It was a mistake I was to regret, for strands of barbed wire tore into the muscles and veins of my left leg, leaving an open wound.

The immediate problem was to deal with that wound. Once back in Madrid, I attended the City Hospital, where, despite the problems arising from casualties of the revolt, a doctor saw me immediately and did all he could with the damage. Having applied the necessary dressings he warned me to keep the limb well exercised, and thought that daily walks undertaken in a vigorous manner would be a good thing. 'Get out of the city,' he said, 'and go for a good, fast stroll down a country road. I may still decide to put that leg in plaster,' and this, a few days later, he did.

On the whole we had had a lucky escape. Eugene had been torn by the thorns, although he had escaped the barbed wire, and although Rodrigo's van had been battered by the Assault Guards he was still able to drive it away next day.

It was at this point that it became clear to us both that the existence of the Red Army poised somewhere in the outer suburbs for its descent upon the capital was the stuff of dreams, and that normality was about to return to the capital; the sight of its citizens walking in its streets with their hands held high would eventually be forgotten. Nevertheless the official State of Alarm was to continue. Armoured cars and even light tanks cruised aimlessly in the suburbs. Places of entertainment suspected of having favoured the old so-called Fascist regime still remained shuttered. No trains ran and public transport outside urban areas had yet to be restored. The Assault Guards, who had spent much of the revolt sheltering in doorways, now made their presence felt, chasing revolutionaries off the scene and pulling down old red flags that had been overlooked. The revolt, it was generally believed, had been within an ace of success and was only, as it seemed at this time, likely to fail through divisions that had risen between the leaders of too many factions.

CHAPTER 9

THE COUNTRY WALK recommended at the hospital had to be put off for a few days, for despite what was generally accepted as the collapse of the revolt, normal life had not been restored. An hour's stroll in the central streets of the capital was still likely to be disturbed by the sound of distant shots. A suicide squad held out for most of a morning in the working-class suburb of Tetuan. A car rammed into a police station after the driver had leapt to safety and the house of a leading right-wing politician was set on fire.

In discussing the matter of a therapeutic walk the people at the hospital suggested the Toledo road, which in view of the fact that the State of Alarm was still in force was presumed to be clear of its normal volume of traffic. Taxis were not included in restrictions on travel so we hired one to take us to an area recommended for its scenery. Once there, we walked for a hundred yards or so, followed in my case by a short rest in the taxi before recommencing the walk.

The walk turned out to be of great interest and provided an opportunity to analyse that sense of the fantastic which the Spanish landscape seldom failed to produce.

I came to the conclusion that this visual effect originates

partly in the dryness of the air which leaves the remotest corners of the plains unsoftened by distance, and in its turn produces an almost eerie feeling of proximity with the very limits of vision. With this went a kind of suppression of irrelevant detail, a directness and evenness of colouring, and something of a stylisation of light and shade in the manner of a travel poster. The hollows and hillocks, and the rare line of poplars, appeared to arrange themselves in rhythmic patterns. The fields reeled away in all directions, forming immaculate designs in pale gold and silver. Summer had long since withered away in a single week, and the sun glittered with chilly brilliance in the dark blue sky.

By turning through a complete circle one could observe every form of agricultural and pastoral activity. In one corner the plains were being ploughed and sown, in another they were winnowing the grain, and in a vineyard they gathered the last of the grapes. Knowing nothing of the southern European agricultural routine, these juxtapositions struck me with surprise.

Villages lay in depressions showing only their rooftops, or capped wide hummocks of grass. They were clean-cut and self-contained, like models in relief maps. Oases of trees marked the spots where there were wells. Each clump concealed a waterwheel where a blindfolded mule turned in circles from morning to night. A herd of black sheep passed across the foreground. My impression was that I could almost have hit one of them with a stone. Yet the illusory distances of Spain had reduced them almost to the size of insects.

A dozen short walks spaced out by lifts in the taxi brought us within sight of the outskirts of Madrid. It looked like an avalanche of sparkling debris that had fallen on the edge of the slopes of the Sierra de Guadarrama, stretching across the northern horizon.

That evening we crossed the bridge leading into the city. Pickets of soldiers with fixed bayonets were stopping and searching all vehicles. A week before the outbreak of the revolt a shipload of the latest American cars had arrived in the capital; a half-mile further on we saw the remains of one of these which had fallen into revolutionary hands and been reduced to a smoking ruin in the middle of the road.

Although some restrictions upon travel remained, Madrid had now reached the end of the official State of Alarm. It was at this time that outbreaks of what might have been seen as neurotic behaviour among the general public became noticeable. This was perhaps to be expected after a situation in which many Madrileños had lived under constant fire for up to five days.

Most extraordinary of these strange temporary phenomena was a sudden mania for drinking animals' blood. This was reported within days of the guns falling silent when queues, comprised almost entirely of middle-class women, gathered at the slaughterhouses every morning carrying receptacles such as bottles and mugs. After selecting an animal whose apparent vitality impressed them, these ladies stood by while it was killed then caught the blood as it spurted from the severed veins and gulped it down on the spot. *ABC* reported that ladies unwilling to risk endangering their social status by joining the blood-drinking queue in person sent a deputy, but the paper pointed out that expert opinion in this matter had warned that the loss of the blood's natural heat would cancel out much of the beneficial effect. We were compelled to confirm by a visit to a slaughterhouse that we were not the victims of rumour, but got no further than the building's gates before we were deterred by a woman on her way out, made terrible by the smile painted by the blood on her lips.

The times, it was clear, were changing and with this grew a fear, in the cities, and especially in Madrid, that time-honoured aspects of Spanish national life were under threat. We were warned by friends made in the last few days of crisis that even bullfighting was now at risk through the closure of the old Plaza de Toros which was to follow a final bullfight. Whether or not closure was inevitable, people were determined to see to it that its end was in every way to be remembered. All the minor complications of normal bullfighting were to be swept aside for this grand occasion, and a single *torero*, generally accepted to be the finest horse rider in the land, was offering a unique performance. He would kill no less than eight bulls, using not a sword but a short lance known as a *rejón* which was thrust into the heart. From beginning to end he was to remain in the saddle. Neither rider nor horse would be protected by padding. There would be no team on foot to aid him in any way. The *rejoneador* was to be Don Antonio Cañero, whose adventurous personality was only equalled by his prowess on horseback, earning him the title of Noble Horseman of Spain.

In its last moments the old ring was packed as never before, largely with a family audience of people of the district with three adults squeezed into a space intended for two, while children were gathered up into parental laps. The ring dated from the beginning of the nineteenth century, before such architecture had suffered elsewhere in Spain from some degeneration, when excesses of money in circulation seemed to have blunted the criteria of taste. In describing the new arena, the newspapers criticised the coldness in the colour of the stone employed by comparison with the comfortable warmth of that used in the old building. One critic considered that the principal aim of those responsible for the new plaza had been to cram as many aficionados into it as humanly possible, and no more than that.

Don Antonio Cañero started off with a characteristic display of horsemanship. He rode a pearly grey Arab whose quality was unmistakable even to the lay eye. Circling the centre of the ring this magnificent horse was first induced to perform a series of bounds with its body almost vertical to the floor of the ring and the hooves of its hind legs possibly a foot clear of the ground. This was followed by a circus performance of delicate sidestepping round the ring in acknowledgment of the almost hysterical plaudits of the crowd.

The first bull entered the ring and Don Antonio changed the Arab for another less showy horse, took a pair of beribboned *banderillas* in his right hand and trotted his horse in front and within feet of the bull. It instantly charged. Its short twinkling legs carried it forward like a battering ram. There was no movement whatever in the head or body. This was a clean unswerving attack with enough weight behind it to demolish a brick wall.

Don Antonio spurred up to the gallop and described a perfect arc, judging the distance so as just to miss the horns, leaning over in the saddle to plant the *banderillas* in the bull's shoulder muscles as it tore past. Feeling the barbs, the bull leapt into the air, tried to turn too quickly, slipped and rolled over in the sand. Everyone laughed. There were *banderillas* hanging from the bull's back now. Blood trickled slowly down the shafts, staining the ribbons and dripping on the sand. With a great convulsion it shook two of them loose. The *rejón* that followed was evidently not thrust deep enough to pierce the heart. There had to be a second and yet a third attempt. The third time Don Antonio was just a fraction of a second out with his timing. As he stabbed down the bull's horns caught the horse's groin and opened up a sagging foot-long gash. Having failed to kill with three thrusts of the *rejón*, etiquette now compelled him to take the matador's *muleta* and sword and finish off the job on foot.

This was easier said than done. Don Antonio's forte was obviously horsemanship. It was evident from his over-emphasised gestures that he was not happy as a matador. Moreover, facing a bull that has previously had half its neck muscles torn from their anchorage by the proddings of the picador, is one thing, and this is what happens in an ordinary bullfight. But a bull that has not been success-fully crippled but most successfully enraged is another, and once again there was a swift splattering of hooves as it made its annihilating charge. Don Antonio lifted the scarlet square of the *muleta* in a *paso do alto* to induce the bull to charge through under his right arm, but this was an animal that failed to conform to the rules of the sport. Catching the matador full in the thighs it lifted him high into the air straddled on its horns. For a moment he was held with arms outstretched in an attitude of crucifixion, and then dashed to the ground. With its legs firmly planted apart and lashing the air with its tail, the bull twisted its head, goring the inanimate form. A few minutes later the attendants carrying Don Antonio came stumbling past us along the *barrera*. It was given out that he was dead.

The rest of the entertainment passed off without a hitch. The seven remaining bulls were successfully reduced, by more or less scientific methods, to shambling impotence and then despatched by regular matadors kept in readiness for such an emergency, three sword-thrusts being necessary on average to finish off each animal.

Seven repetitions of the same ritual transformed revulsion into tedium. The skilful pass of the cloak by which the bull's strength is worn down is the most attractive part of the business to the average outsider. But this has no great appeal for the expert crowd. They are impatient of this kind of thing. It exasperates them if the matador plays the bull too long before giving it the death thrust. In both Eugene's and my cases revulsion reigned supreme, and when in the following years I have been invited by Spanish friends to join them in their appreciation of such spectacles, I have always been ready with an excuse for avoiding them.

CHAPTER 10

WITH THE END of the official State of Alarm, it was time at last to make what arrangements we could for the continuation of our much delayed pilgrimage to Seville. Train travel between the capital and most destinations was still difficult, but a number of long-distance buses were already on the road, many of them presumably going in a southern direction, and we were recommended to choose one of these. To our surprise, however, no direct route to the south had been opened and the first stages of a journey to Seville would carry the traveller some seventy miles in a north-westerly direction to Salamanca, from which more or less direct routes to the south had, so they said, been opened. In a way this turned out to be no bad thing, although we were warned that the quality of these indirect approaches to the south left something to be desired in the way of comfort – and even security.

The bus that went to Salamanca at half past seven in the morning seemed at first sight a foolhardy sort of vehicle to travel in. It was an ancient though massive Leyland six-wheeler that, even though parked upon what appeared a perfectly level road leaned slightly to one side as we inspected it. There were whole areas of painted-over hammer marks on the wings and the body where the ravages left by minor collisions had been straightened out. Worst of all six tyres were down to the canvas. Several women passengers who were in mourning crossed themselves before getting aboard, but this being a custom in Catholic countries, it had no special significance.

At the last moment before starting the driver and an official of the bus company had an argument about the tyres. In the end two new ones were hastily put on the back wheels, leaving only four on the point of bursting. The driver, pointing out that he would have to drive at fifty miles an hour most of the way to reach Salamanca in scheduled time, said that he would have felt happier with the new tyres at the front. The company man regretted that they could not see their way to accommodate him in this. In their opinion the front tyres, having less weight to carry than the back, were good for another two hundred miles, or even three hundred with luck. They compromised by having two modestly worn tyres slung up on top of the bus, which, it was agreed, were only to be used in case of a burst.

In the course of this debate, allusion was made to big losses that had to be considered. Every now and again they lost a bus. This was obvious later from the sight of charred wreckage at the bottom of ravines or piled up against the big rocks at the sides of the road. There was a notice telling you how much you could claim in case of loss sustained by accident. The sums promised were not large. Somewhere about five or six pounds in most cases. Our trip to Salamanca seemed at this point a bit of an adventure, but it turned out to be a rewarding one, for we were to experience places and people of the kind that we had no idea could exist in the remotest areas of Europe, let alone Spain.

*   *   *

The Sierra de Guadarrama, which had to be crossed, proved in a way to be the most spectacular mountain range either of us had ever seen. This was largely due to the sensation evoked of total isolation. It had escaped human invasion to remain a region of almost total emptiness, with its lower slopes covered with a jumble of coloured rocks. Our exhaust thundered and rumbled as we hustled through narrow, rocky valleys, dislodging flocks of jackdaws and doves from the trees like alternating avalanches of soot and snow. Falcons, buzzards and even eagles had possession of almost every telegraph pole. Some eagles made a motion at our approach as if to launch themselves into the air, but by the time a decision had been reached it was too late; we were past and, folding their wings, they settled down again to the waiting game. A flock of some fifty pigmy deer divided to canter through the valley with us, on each side of the bus. Happily the driver was an ardent admirer of nature. Although he had done these trips almost every day for years, he was still under the spell of the mountains and sometimes shot out an arm to indicate scenes whose grandeur had never palled upon him.

More remarkably perhaps, he was extremely critical of the occasional invasion of modern times. For already the city was reaching out its tentacles towards the mountains, befouling their skirts with ribbon building. Here and there chalets and hispano-mauresque villas strove to combine feudal aloofness with modern accessibility by being built on the summits of many of the less precipitous eminences. Once in a while a soap advertisement painted in tar appeared on a boulder, and the first of the roadhouses had tidied away the wildness of its chosen spot.

Salamanca, most splendid of Spanish cities, awaited us, the great red towers of its universities, cathedrals, colleges and convents leaning against the sky. Its doctors, deacons and professors bustled through the streets, and it boasted the nation's most dignified prostitutes, composing poetry and peering hopefully through the windows of the Gran Café damaged regretfully in the revolt and as yet not wholly rectified.

This, as it happened, was market day, when the normal ease and tranquillity of the town is a little disturbed by the presence of country folk who crowd in to dispose of their produce and enjoy, even at a distance, the relaxations and entertainments of city life. In doing so they provided an unusual tourist attraction, for many of them were from the most backward and poverty-stricken area of the whole country and were even beginning, on these grounds, to make an appearance as curiosities in the brochures distributed by the local Patronato de Turismo.

Articles had appeared in the press voicing the opinion that some of the strange country folk inhabiting the roadless undeveloped areas of the east of the city could be the descendants of such prehistoric tribes as the Visigoths, and on learning that Grunwald, the German in charge of the Patronato de Turismo, happened to be an anthropologist, we called there to hear his views on this matter.

'These people,' said Grunwald, 'are just peasants living under impossible conditions in such places as Las Hurdes where things are as bad as they can be, and the land so poor that nothing grows on it. Whatever they may tell you here they suffer from semi-starvation. They're out of reach of medical aid and, of course, of education. The tourists who are taken to see them are told to bring leftovers of food along and they feed them like animals. The primitives, as they're called, are told to make funny faces to go with their thanks. It's easy to talk about Vandals and

Visigoths and that's all part of the tourist attraction. They fixed up a tour, "See the Wild Men of the Woods. Snack lunch included – 100 pesetas."

'For these people,' Grunwald said, 'Salamanca on market day is heaven. They stand in line to grab meat ordered by the inspectors to be given to the dogs, and the outer leaves of the cabbages. There's a character here they call El Panadero – the Baker – because he collects all the stale bread and carries a sackful of it back to be shared among his friends. He's the one whose picture appeared on the cover of *El Tiempo* when they called him "Our Prehistoric Man". If you'd like to make his acquaintance I'll send for him. He's happy to be taken notice of, but you won't understand whatever he has to say.'

Grunwald sent an employee to find El Panadero, who returned with him in a matter of minutes. He was a small man with a wide, flat nose, narrowed eyes and thick lips. Black down covered the lower part of his face. Grunwald had half a loaf in readiness, and taking it El Panadero's lips seemed to writhe.

'He wants to smile like we do,' Grunwald said, 'but he can't.'

El Panadero grunted softly, stuffed a crust into his mouth and began to chew. 'Perhaps that's the way the Visigoths talked,' Grunwald said. 'I've tried hard but I can't understand him. Anyway, he's a nice man and I like him, and he's happy. That's the main thing.'

Almost immediately after leaving Salamanca, a main road to the west and to the town of Guarda over the Portuguese frontier crosses a vast swampy plain, in places more than a hundred miles wide, with one of the lowest populations in Europe, in fact numerically less than that of a single small Portuguese town. This is because according to the season much of this great spread of grass is under water, and with little to support human life beyond the modest requirements of the occupants of some twenty of Europe's tiniest villages. As would be suspected, the members of these communities have been compelled to develop extraordinary strategies to cope with the disadvantages of their surroundings in which incessant rainfall keeps the ground sodden the year round. This, it seems likely – as in the case of El Panadero – may have benefited the possessors of exceptionally large feet.

With the intention of discovering whatever it might be that this sodden landscape had to offer we hired a jeep in Salamanca, and after two miles along the main road to Zamora in the north turned left into an extremely narrow track along the bank of the Rio Tormes, covering a difficult and sometimes hazardous twenty-five miles before being obliged to turn back. What faced us from this point on were marshes.

Two features of this drive were exceptional. One was the rain, which started three miles out of Salamanca, and continued as if automatically switched on by our presence until the end of the road. The second was the lively colour of these floods in which blues, greens and yellows intermingled as if stirred by currents in the depths. A sharp, watery smell was released, we believed, by the mud and gas from a million exploding bubbles. Grunwald mentioned that the water was believed to possess substantial therapeutic qualities, adding that dogs allowed to drink nothing else often became more sexually active.

Where there was dry land growing nothing but brilliant grass, the primitives of Salamanca had dug out their caves. These, often chosen by preference for human habitation, are virtually a speciality of Spain. There are enormous communities of cave dwellers down in Guadix in the far south and, as we had seen at Tudela, on the road to Zaragoza, several thousand citizens had chosen to live beneath the earth's surface, many of them in reasonably sophisticated surroundings. Neither the lifestyles nor life span of these people were affected by the absence of blue sky overhead. Caves hollowed out of the earth were clearly cheaper to construct and obviously easier in a cold climate than houses exposed to the winds. Nevertheless Grunwald admitted that the so-called primitives of Salamanca would be lucky to reach two-thirds of the urban man's life span. 'It's cold in winter in those holes in the ground and you need more to eat than if you live in a house. Starvation doesn't come into it. El Panadero eats more than an urban man. He eats as much as the Archbishop of Salamanca, but it's the wrong kind of food.'

Grunwald had been looking into the question of the best possible route to take to the south. 'Only one thing matters,' I said. 'That is to get to Seville with the minimum loss of time.'

'I'm sorry, my dear friends,' Grunwald said. 'I was just this moment on the phone to some business contacts and they all agree that your best hope is to go via Portugal.'

'Portugal? Why on earth?' I said. 'It would take us hundreds of miles out of our way.'

Grunwald shrugged. 'Well not quite that, but it would certainly be a bit of a detour. The news is that the State of Alarm will almost certainly be reinstated. Most of the buses are off the road already and trains to the south are likely to be delayed. It would be slow going via Portugal, but the thing is you'd get there. I forgot to mention that a general strike has been called at Caceres which you'd have to pass through on the direct Spanish route. One of the good things about Portugal is that they don't have strikes.'

Eugene wanted to know how long a detour through Portugal might add to the journey, and Grunwald told him perhaps a week. 'I'm afraid it's one of those places,' he said, 'where time seems less important than it does to us. I put in the best part of a year there and I found out by the end of that time that I'd stopped worrying too. Travelling by train in Portugal can be quite amusing, in any case. Troubadors, if you can imagine it, come aboard to sing to you. I had to go down to Coimbra last year. They didn't bring the drinks along as usual and one of the passengers said he was thirsty. A peasant woman who was nursing her baby said, "Sorry about that. How about a drop of my milk?" They all thought it a great joke. That's how the Portuguese are. Great people and full of fun. You're going to fall for them.'

'I know we will,' Eugene told him. 'The trouble is my father is paying our fares and he doesn't have a sense of humour.'

'All the better that it's so cheap,' Grunwald said. 'The Portuguese travel whenever they can because it's supposed to be good for the liver. Half the time they don't know where they're going, or when they'll get there. The slower the train the better it is for the digestion, they tell you. Perhaps I shouldn't mention this, but when and if you go to Portugal you'll find that the Salamanca–Porto Express averages six and two-thirds miles an hour for the journey.'

'I can't believe it,' I said. 'Surely you must be joking.'

'It's far from a joke,' Grunwald said, 'nor does it break the record. They're experimenting with a diesel electric train somewhere up in the north which so far for a long journey has only averaged two miles per hour.'

Next day we took the train for Barca de Alba on the Portuguese frontier. This, so far as we could see, carried no passengers other than ourselves and a few Portuguese labourers, whose standard of living was so low that they could actually work and save a little money in Spain to take home with them. Three of these displayed, with a touch of pride, ulcers on their arms that had developed from small wounds that had turned septic – probably, we guessed, as a result of malnutrition. Within minutes of setting out, the golden steppes of Spain had faded away and the landscape became green with intensive cultivation. At this our fellow passengers crowded to the window and smiled rapturously as they pointed out for our benefit the first vines and cabbages of Portugal.

At Barca de Alba we boarded the Portuguese train that awaited us. We were greeted by a group of mummers with faces painted in medieval style who muttered what we were assured was a welcome between outbursts of what seemed to us sinister laughter.

The train was even worse than the Spanish one, with compartments both cramped and sharply rectangular, plus doorways so narrow that a stout passenger had some difficulty in squeezing through. The carriages were high above the tracks and since there was no platform, elderly passengers – several of them sick – were surrendered to the desperate struggle of fellow travellers attempting to lift or drag them aboard. The compartments were always crowded, and we were obliged in the end to squat with our legs curled up among collections of baggage piled on the floor.

The little we could see of the scenery came as a disappointment. The mountainous slopes among which the Douro wound its way were so thoroughly cultivated as to render the river as insignificant in appearance as an irrigation ditch. Even the tongues of rock projecting into the water had in many cases been covered with soil and planted with vegetables, thus the landscape had been reduced to an enormous, rolling cabbage patch. Trivial, and to us even boring, the outlook was one that filled our fellow travellers with excitement. There was always competition for a place at the window and this was solved in what seemed to us an extraordinary fashion. A queue of three or four passengers would form and the viewing time for each checked by a watch that set off an alarm at the termination of what seemed to be some five minutes. The passenger at the head of the queue would then, if slow in his withdrawal, be taken resolutely by the shoulders by whoever followed him and thrust irresistibly aside. It was clearly a regular procedure, and taken in perfectly good part.

Apart from the application of the law of the survival of the fittest to the initial processes of catching and boarding the train, relations once the journey was under way were cordial. Conversation was general and food communally shared to the last pullet's wing and crust of saffron-flavoured bread. Having brought no food with us this was a custom that caused us much embarrassment. This was the time when we were to learn that all the old courtesies and primitive social mechanisms surviving in Spain only as flowers of speech were still in everyday operation in Portugal. When a peasant on a Spanish train pulls out his bread and sausage and invites you to join him the single word employed is '*Gusta?*' and the conventional answer, '*Que aproveche*', besides meaning 'good appetite', also implies polite refusal. This is not the case in Portugal, and in these first encounters we were to realise that faced occasionally with such a refusal the offerer showed signs of feeling hurt.

Unfortunately although we could just about read a Portuguese newspaper, the rapid and confident gabble of the peasant world had nothing in common – as we had hoped it would – with the clear-cut verbalisms of Spain, and we were only too often reduced to mime.

There was only one incident among the many communal jokes and discussions which we could appreciate. This was when an old lady, being called hastily from the lavatory for one reason or other, succeeded in losing her drawers. We were coming to the station where she would have to get out and the impropriety of climbing down the steep steps in her condition filled her with panic. Her frenzied individual appeals to the other occupants of the carriage set everybody in fits of mirth. Only when we had come to the station and the performance was over did someone produce the missing garment and return it to her out of the window.

CHAPTER 11

WE INTERRUPTED OUR intended journey down through the length of Portugal and then to Seville on account of a highly sensational witchcraft murder in a village near Porto.

This had taken place in Marco do Canavezes, where a woman had been burned to death in the presence of a considerable crowd in accordance with the rites of the Book of St Cyprian, a species of manual dealing with the black arts, still on sale, we were told, in most village post offices.

Her neighbours believed that this young woman was occupied by an evil spirit, for which the only remedy was death by fire. According to the book, however, all was not lost, for in the scriptures according to St Cyprian exposure to fire was in reality no more than a curative exercise, after which the victim would be born again, arising from the ashes, as the book put it, 'as pure as a white lily, or dove'.

It was this triumphant conclusion that the villagers were said to have waited for, possibly with fading hopes, as they stared down at the remnants of the holocaust at the dead end of a village street, and quoting, as they did, the book's instructions when brought before the judge, it was impossible to convince them that they had been involved in what the law insisted was murder.

A few days later the police arrested the 'Witch of Caudal', a local celebrity under whose guidance the precepts of the Book of St Cyprian were administered. Innumerable illiterate peasants had contributed their tiny sums to her revenue, but the names of magistrates, bankers and generals were also to be found on her books. The newspapers published a photograph of her taken at a reception in one of the embassies in Lisbon at the moment of raising a glass in acknowledgment of good wishes. She had at first been punished by an official rebuke.

A doctor who spoke good English happened to be staying at the hotel and we talked about the burning over a drink.

'Does the poverty you see everywhere here have any bearing on happenings like this?' Eugene wanted to know.

'In a way undoubtedly,' our friend said. 'All these villages are poor – and in a way deprived – although not desperately so. The suicide rate is high, but lower I would say, for example, than in a Balkan country. I mention this because in a curious sort of way this is beginning to look more like suicide than murder.'

'What gave you that idea?' I asked him.

'Well, in the first place our peasants don't kill each other, but there are almost epidemics of suicide.'

'It's something I would never have suspected.'

'It puzzles us, too. It may be a matter of loss of self-esteem. They see themselves as failures. The victim in this case, for example, had lost her lover and her confidence collapsed. She began to talk about being persecuted by an evil spirit to which she ascribed her troubles. The next thing she's heard to say is that she's tired of life. "I'm going," she said, "I've had enough of it. Make sure that you're at least here to help me when I go."'

'To a dreadful end,' I said. 'But why did she choose such a fearful way of doing the thing?'

'Because for her it was a triumph of a kind. She was going to be the star performer in a tragedy that the whole country would hear about. Tourists would come in buses to see the place where she'd chosen to die. By this time she probably saw herself as a heroine.'

'I'm sure you're right.'

'The fact is that this book is the *vade mecum* of suicides. They're all hoping for an easy way out. We have to remember that on the whole these people are a soft-hearted lot. There's even a recipe for a dose to be given to felons to quieten them down before execution.' He paused to give further thought to the possibilities. 'She may have been blind drunk when it came to the crunch,' he said. 'Let's hope that's the way it was.'

'Is it true,' I asked, 'that there's been talk of a memorial plaque to mark the spot?'

The doctor barked a scornful laugh. 'That wouldn't go down well even with tourists. No, this has to be forgotten. Nobody's going to make the pilgrimage to this dull little place just for the kick of seeing where they burned that poor, silly girl. Memorial plaques are out,' he said.

Marco de Canavezes, we decided, was not to be missed. The doctor put us in touch with a car hire firm which supplied the aged Fiat that carried us through flowering valleys and eagle-encircled peaks down to Canavezes. We stopped to gaze down on the pink roofs gleaming among the trees over the Sousa River. A hill road curved down and through to the small square where the tragedy had been staged. The village was poor with tiny houses built on its outskirts, sometimes appearing to consist of a single room. Women in black squeezed past us along the narrow street. Leaving the car as soon as we could, we continued on foot down to the centre, to which, said the notice, only horse-drawn traffic was admitted.

We had been recommended by our friend to announce our presence to the police, but a notice tacked to the station door informed us that the officer in charge was away for that day. We were later to learn that he was shared with other villages.

Fortunately the doctor had arranged for us to meet an ex-patient of his, a tall pink-faced young man in his early twenties who blinked nervously when informed of the purpose of our visit. He put aside whatever he was doing to talk to us, having first pulled down the blind over his window. There was some difficulty because the man spoke only Portuguese, but a friend was fetched who translated what he had to say into Spanish.

'Did you know her?' I asked.

'In the village,' he said, 'we all know each other.'

'Do you believe she was possessed by an evil spirit?'

He winced, and drew his fingers across his mouth as if to wipe away something clinging to his lips. A moment of silence followed before he said, 'I cannot reply to this.'

'Why do you think they burned this poor woman?'

'They blamed her for the plague that killed many people two years ago.'

'Plagues are not caused by evil spirits,' I told him, 'but the dirt in the big cities, and the sickness that spreads from it.'

He nodded, as if in agreement, although I believed that his opinion remained the same.

'When they took this woman from her house,' he said, 'she was laughing, so they put a gag in her mouth. After that they carried her to the place where the stake was set up and tied her to it. They covered her face with a mask. The priest was there to pronounce the forgiveness of the Church and to frustrate the devil by renaming her Gabriel, after the angel. All the people who went with her were religious persons who were concerned with her acceptance into the world of those who are saved. The church bell was tolled three times, the people covered their eyes, and the fire was lit. Those who attended the ceremony shook hands with each other. A few women wept.'

'Did you stay?'

'No one was allowed to leave, but many turned their heads away. You see, we Portuguese are compassionate by nature. Many covered their faces to hide their tears.'

The next day we took a slow train to Coimbra which proved to be a city of tea shops and beggars, but above all it was known for eccentric happenings in which it was conceivable that its citizens took some pride. The latest story, related by the waitress in our first tea shop, was of a man who had put on wings, leapt into the air from a low cliff and broken both legs. There was a disputed claim as to whether or not a priest displayed the stigmata and that day's paper reported that a house consisting of nine rooms built one on top of the other had just collapsed.

Coimbra had been put on the tourist map at the beginning of the century by the visit of the celebrated Prince of Lichnovsky who was there in the first instance for treatment of 'a complaint of the loins', for which it was said that the town's physicians were still renowned. Sufferers from this ailment must have flocked to its hospitals and clinics and Lichnovsky's relief at their efficiency may have been reflected in his description of the town. Of it, the most distinguished traveller of his day said, 'Nothing similar to its beauty and magnificence have I gazed upon in all Europe.' Of the neighbouring forest of Bussaco, he said, 'I feel myself wafted away in the marvellous and very ancient wooded regions of the Orient.' This ecstatic description was reproduced in a booklet published by the Portuguese Touring Club, which, however, ignored Lichnovsky's recommendation of the forest as 'exceptionally suitable for romantic exploits of an intimate character'.

It was a town possessing not only the traces of past splendours, but one that had even managed to preserve echoes of a class system inherited from Victorian times. Its many beggars were fed publicly by splendidly attired persons of social standing who remained scrupulously aloof from physical contact with the poor they were helping. These beggars were even given tiny sums of money by servants, who managed to maintain a certain aloofness from the process too, some covering their nostrils with their hands. An up-to-date cinema had just opened and its patrons were besieged by supplicants who, while managing to ignore servants offering scraps of bread, knelt down in the street to thank their distant benefactors at the back of the crowd.

The news reaching us here was depressing indeed. We were now committed – with all arrangements made – to travelling the full length of what remained of Portugal down to Villa Real de Santo Antonio on its south coast, and at this point crossing the River Guadiana to reach Ayamonte on the Spanish frontier. Now, without the slightest warning, came the crushing news that the Spanish State of Alarm was back – if anything in a more threatening form. The town of Ayamonte – across the river from Villa Real – was on the frontier of the Rio Tinto mining area with the largest coal and iron mines in Spain. Here heavy fighting between revolutionary miners and the Spanish Army had once again broken out. Thus the ferry to Spain had been suspended indefinitely and a special permit was required from the Spanish Governor of Huelva to cross the river. Was there any hope, we asked our travel agent, after this appalling news, of crossing over to Seville? His reply was, 'In our country all such crises are fluid. Today promises no solution, but that does not mean that tomorrow you cannot travel. Then again, do not let us be over-optimistic. At the last time of such a disruption the frontier was shut for a month.'

The next time we saw our friend at the travel agency we armed ourselves with sweets to curry favour with the irresistible children who had cordoned off the approach to the entrance. He listened with sympathy to what we had to tell him before waving a hand in protest.

'All this,' he said, 'boils down to one simple and inescapable fact, namely that you have to persuade a person of influence in Villa Real to take you under his wing.'

'And how do we set about doing that?'

He sighed, 'In the usual way, I'm afraid.'

'You mean we make it worth their while?'

'Exactly that,' he said. 'And remember that whoever you talk to about this will assume that you expect him to work for you, and that the work will be tricky – furthermore that this man will have a necessitous family to feed.'

'Now I understand. And what will it cost?'

'Well, say fifty dollars, or the equivalent in pounds. Each of you, I mean. Escudos aren't accepted.'

'And you think that's likely to do the trick?'

'If anything can,' he said. 'When do you want to go?'

'As soon as it can possibly be arranged.'

'If you can afford it I strongly recommend first class. Otherwise it's like being in a war. I can get you forty per cent off the advertised rates.'

'Don't bother about that,' I told him. 'We'll be writing about the experience.'

'As you please. It'll certainly be just that.

'A word of advice,' he added. 'Take American cigarettes with you. You can use them when you can't use money. The story is that they put shavings from the leather factory into the local brand. I'll give the fellow at Villa Real a buzz and tell him to expect you. By the way, the guy has a sister you might find interesting, so take a bottle of Coty along. Better to have two friends in court than one, and every little helps.'

CHAPTER 12

THE JOURNEY FROM Coimbra to Lisbon, our first stop on the way, took eight hours. The engine of our train bore the mark 'Manchester 1890', and the carriages had probably been considered luxurious at about that time. The trip gave us some idea of how our grandfathers had travelled. There was no corridor, but this deficiency by no means impeded free circulation between compartments. The ticket collector and the passengers, including women in voluminous skirts, just scaled the low barriers dividing up the carriages.

The attractions of the towns through which we passed were advertised in splendidly *azulejo*-tiled tableaux on the station walls. We recognised the names of several health resorts we had spotted in the press, and not only minor complaints of the loins came in for mention, but in one case a lightning cure for syphilis had been frankly included.

We were travelling in a compartment full of peasant girls who were going into service in Lisbon. Several of them, as they told us with no evidence of sorrow, had said goodbye to their families for the last time, and were being taken by their employer straight out to Brazil. Their parents had loaded them with eatables, and these were stacked in careful piles along the seats, while the girls remained standing throughout the journey, clustered round the windows. Some had never been on a train before. From the moment they got on board until we drew into the station at Lisbon, they held their tickets clutched in their hands. Every time a train going in the opposite direction rushed by, they flung up their arms to shield their faces and crouched down in terror.

Apart from watching the landscape fly by the girls sang *jotas* in shrill, powerful voices, with occasional outbursts of laughter at the introduction of a passage of salacious wit. After the first hour or so they became exceedingly friendly. One of them had decided to change the position of some heavy luggage, and on being complimented by Eugene on her impressive strength she rolled up her sleeve to display her forearm, saying, 'Just take a grip of this.'

We changed trains at Lisbon and thereafter were to encounter poverty of the kind that neither of us had experienced before. This, as we saw it, was a result of unfairly distributed resources, illustrated by emphatic social divisions and the side-by-side display of desperate poverty and extreme wealth. The Portuguese south, outside the towns, illustrated a degree of misery that was limitless and unchanging. This advertised its presence, for example, in tiny village houses with the minutest of doors and no windows or chimney. In areas of the Algarve, in the far south, we were assured that about half the rural houses consisted of a single room. On several occasions we saw a man walking in the street wearing a single shoe. In answer to our questioning we were told, 'That is his stock in trade,' meaning that it was for sale and that in cases of desperate poverty shoes – although not necessarily in pairs – were offered for sale.

The simple experiences of Portugal could be adventurous. The train stopped wherever it was called upon to do so – often by little groups of girls on their way to shop in the nearest town, who would wave their thanks to the driver before climbing aboard. This, indeed, was a cheap and cheerful life, and by this time we had picked up enough of the language to be instantly included in these peasant groups. Each group came prepared with two-gallon stone jars of wine which were passed over the barriers from compartment to compartment. The grapes, they told us, were sold in a Lisbon shop at a penny per kilogram, and the wine – carried with them wherever they went – cost two pence per litre. Third-class travel by trains here was a splendid adventure, with our relationship immediately cemented for the continuation of the journey by the almost sacramental procedure of taking wine together.

Another party of servant girls formed part of the congenial group in the third-class carriage. No doubt put at their ease by the wine, the girls began to examine our clothing with frequent cries of admiration and wonder. We failed to correspond with their previous opinions of how members of the Anglo-Saxon race should appear and behave. One girl who had worked for an English family in Lisbon had, until this moment, understood that all Britishers – just as her employers had been – were ginger-headed. These cheerful, muscular, uninhibited ladies, it turned out, were bound for Praia da Rocha in the far south, an unfinished resort spoken of hopefully, but with eyes sometimes raised to the heavens, as the future Portuguese Riviera. At all events, the girls agreed the wages – equivalent of three shillings per week – were good, and if the worst came to the worst they could always walk home in a matter of two or three days. They laughed and clapped their hands.

From Lisbon down through Estremadura and Alentejo the peasantry kept out of sight when not slaving in the fields. Then down in the Algarve, drama returned like the reopening of a great play. A golden flush had spread through the landscape, and with the renewed beauty of the earth its people had recovered a little of the mobility destroyed by the masters of the great estates. The women-folk appeared at the entrances to their houses like players on stage as the curtain is lifted, and there were times when we were reminded of the poses of classical statuary. We passed through the outskirts of a village where images were being carried in procession and the male celebrants raised their hats to the train. Now clear of the bleached pastures and turnip fields, the colour had flooded back into the scene, with the red earth turned by the ploughs, the black pine-forest and a sky full of white cranes. Deer browsing as calm as cows in these empty places sprinted away from the terror of the train. A falcon dropped like a stone from the sky and a fox was flushed from its cover within a half-dozen yards of the track. We rattled slowly southwards as the last of many deer vanished from sight and the first of the cowboys trotted into view.

CHAPTER 13

SUDDENLY, AT THE end of a long day, we had come to the end of Portugal. Its colour, its mystery and its splendid wilderness were no more. Forests had become managed woodlands, rivers were bridged, villages were encircled by cabbage patches and advertisements for coffee were stencilled on walls. What was to be expected of Villa Real de Santo Antonio, we had enquired of our fellow travellers. They had shrugged their shoulders, preferring evidently not to be the bearers of ill-tidings.

Despite the grandiose name it appeared more as an untidy village with dogs disputing the rubbish in its streets, and most of the inhabitants looked like criminal suspects temporarily free while awaiting imprisonment in chains or deportation. The problem facing normal inhabitants at this moment was the closure of the frontier, provoking, as we were to discover, a species of claustrophobia. We had been met by a member of the council who led the way to a Portuguese version of a Nissen hut that was to be placed at our disposal.

Following our inspection of this, I put the question, 'Do foreign tourists come here?'

His reply was, 'Sometimes earlier in the year, yes – but at this time the weather is not good.'

'How do they occupy themselves?'

'The café is open two nights out of three,' he said. 'On Saturday evenings there is a cinema show. Those wishing to stay on for a repeat of the programme must book a day in advance.'

'And are there other attractions?' I asked.

'When it is possible to visit Spain, day trips are available, but now with the State of Alarm these are no longer possible and it has become a little more dull.'

At least we discovered Villa Real possessed a public telephone and we got through to Gordon Street for the first time in a week. Ernesto came on the line. 'How was it then? You go to Seville?'

'No. This is Portugal. We're still on the way.'

'How much longer this take?'

'Not long, Ernesto. Didn't you hear? The Spanish closed the frontier. Some more fighting started up. As soon as they let us through we'll be there in a day.'

'You call me then, huh? You tell me how things are. I am waiting.'

A notice left on the hut door informed us that we must present ourselves at the office of the Chief of the International Police who we found in his cabin down on the waterfront, thumbing through a collection of mug shots of wanted criminals before pasting them in an album.

He was most affable as well as consolatory over our situation. The enemy in Villa Real, he told us, and as we had already supposed, was boredom. There was very little to occupy body or mind. Undesirable persons attempted to take refuge here, he said, and two prisons had been made ready to deal with them. A prisoner could choose to pay twenty-five escudos a day for a higher category of incarceration. For the ordinary lock-up you paid nothing, but, said the Police Chief, it had to be admitted that conditions were not good.

In a speech punctuated by hearty laughs and recommendations to a fatalistic acceptance of the inevitable, the Chief saw nothing for it in our case but a return to Lisbon, where he had no doubt that we could get a boat back to England. It was a point of view underlined at that moment by the sound of distant gunfire.

He described the case of two other stranded foreigners who at that moment were to be seen approaching us across the otherwise deserted waterfront. The short one, he told us, was a recently released Polish criminal who had been given three days to leave the country, the other a somewhat mysterious German whose visa was about to expire and who was faced with the possible alternative of joining the Pole or waiting in the rat-infested non-paying prison. This by no means affected the Police Chief's social attitude towards them, and while we were discussing the immediate future of all involved they dropped in for a chat and a smoke. There were introductions, cigarettes were passed round, and there was a general conversation about the quality of the film shown the evening before.

After this the Pole and the German went off while the Chief indicated by a gesture that he wished us to stay. I began to suspect that he was a lonely man. He had no objection to talking about himself, and he told us that he had studied criminology at Coimbra, mistakenly as he now believed, as it had provided little of the excitement he had expected. The motives of safe breakers could not possibly have less to do with the skills called for in keeping an eye on a national frontier, and he readily admitted that so far as he was concerned life's battle was one against boredom. Take the case of the German, he said. He was travelling on a forged passport, yet proved upon examination to be a statistician who was visiting the area in search of rare medicinal plants. The Pole had actually murdered somebody and, having admitted that he found real criminals more interesting than normal members of the community, it was clear that the Chief was attracted like a moth to the flame by the drama of this man's life.

'The Spanish situation,' the Chief said, 'has provided a little excitement in our dull existences, but even the Spanish cannot go on fighting each other for ever. Any day now the frontier will open up again and we'll be checking shopkeepers from Huelva down here on three-day all-in holiday trips. So what do we do to liven things up?' asked the Chief, appealing like a beggar with outstretched hands to his audience. 'Students from Faro Conventual Academy are coming over to sing Songs of Praise to us next week. There must be some way we can return to real life.'

Later in the day Security HQ Coimbra came through on the phone to the Chief with the news that in future foreigners arriving without visas would be deported. 'They made up their minds at last,' the Chief said.

'So that's the end of our two friends,' I suggested.

'Inevitably,' he said. 'And not too soon.'

'So when's this likely to happen?'

'As soon as anything does in this country. Remember the frontier's still closed and there's no sign of the Spanish changing their minds.'

'What does the frontier consist of?' Eugene asked. 'Some sort of wall, or fence?'

'No, it's the further bank of the Guadiana River,' the Chief explained. 'The Spanish have frontier posts, and patrol it with searchlights at night.'

'But do they really manage to keep the foreigners out?'

Eugene wondered aloud, and the Chief shook his head.

'They do their best,' he said, 'but the fact is there's a constant stream crossing over.'

'Why should that be, with all the trouble in Spain?'

'Foreigners come here because it's cheap. They stay in the best hotels and pay what they would in village inns in their own country. In Portugal they can afford champagne with every meal. This is the cheapest country in Europe.'

'You're probably right,' I told him.

'But the trouble is nothing exciting ever happens. In Spain, as we all know, the reverse is the case. Cross the frontier to Huelva and you have about a one in ten chance of getting your brains blown out. Remarkably enough, some people seem ready to take the risk.'

'But all the same the river frontier idea doesn't work,' I said.

'It works down here at the river's mouth with a Spanish sentry every two hundred metres, but all you have to do is to get someone to drive you upstream, say forty-odd kilometres as far as San Lucar, where there are no posts at all, and get a boatman to row you across.'

CHAPTER 14

THE MOOD IN the café that evening was subdued. The lady in charge of the business (generally regarded as the only pretty woman in Villa Real) had been tempted away to join the staff of what was suspected of being a brothel. With this loss, all the services offered by the café fell into decline, and, worst of all, the food had become inedible.

Surprisingly, in view of the disappointing news, the Chief calling in for his evening brandy and snack seemed more than usually optimistic, despite having decided to surrender a plate of eggs, Albufeira-style, to the dogs waiting at the door. 'The deportations are going ahead after all,' he said. 'No problem. It looks like being easier than expected, and quite a break so far as I'm concerned. Why don't you come along too? Assuming you haven't changed your minds about Spain, there's no easier way.'

'Sounds like wonderful news,' I said. 'One way or another, as I told you, we have to get to Seville.'

'We lead dull lives,' the Chief said. 'For once here's a chance of a little excitement, with no risk to anyone.'

'Is this your original idea?' I asked. 'The one about driving up the N122 to Sanlucar and then crossing the river.'

'No,' he said. 'That's too far and too complicated. This

isn't half the distance. We stay on the N122 but only as far as the Beliche River which flows into the Guadiana. With luck we'll find a boatman on the river to take us across to the far shore. At this point you're in Spanish territory with a cart-track leading to the main Huelva road. There's plenty of local traffic. With luck you'll be in Huelva tonight.'

'What happens to the deportees?'

'That's up to you. Probably better to dump them as soon as possible. Four people travelling together attract more attention than two.'

Next morning the police van was under our window at dawn – that sleepy and slow-moving hour in south Portugal, imbued with the regeneration of memory and the sounds of things past. The Chief was buoyed with high spirits and the promise of even the mildest of adventures. The deportees were crammed into the back; unnecessarily handcuffed for the occasion, they viewed the outside world with indifference.

'So far, so good,' the Chief said, and a backwards jerk of the head suggested the promise of partial victory. 'Now all that matters is whether we shall have the good luck to find a boat . . . Well, we shall see.'

The N122 went straight ahead, plunging resolutely into the flatlands where human purpose – perhaps from fear of invaders from Spain – appeared largely to have been abandoned. Only the great medieval pile of the fortress, Castro Marim, had survived, and perhaps even defeated Spanish incursions. Or possibly the freebooters from Spain found little inducement here to persist in their invasions. This was territory long-since deserted, and in the morning shadows the great castle shared with a single buffalo a landscape of water, mists and sky. It was less than an hour to the Beliche River, which uncoiled through innumerable curves down from the mountains of the north to straighten itself finally among the sheep south of Azinhal.

Our relief when this small town came distantly into view was very great. Greater still was the sight of the Beliche bridge and of the promised boatman and his boat tied up by the bank where the river curved away into thin forest, with a glimpse between the tree trunks of the distant mountains of Spain. We clambered down a slight elevation for a better view of the river. Below us a great spread of smooth water appeared to slide rather than flow through sun-scorched terrain stretching to the far horizon. In this prospect, and at that moment only, floating bunches of leaves indicated the speed and direction of the current.

The boatman greeted us with huge enthusiasm although obviously as a matter of habit, turning his head slightly away when he spoke. It was a tic clearly induced by a disfiguring birthmark on his left cheek, and I was reminded that it was the compassionate habit of the rural Portuguese to grant such jobs as his to persons suffering from physical defects.

The Chief explained our presence and asked whether any problems were likely to arise in the crossing to Spain. The boatman assured us that none would. 'In fact we might even run into a taxi driver from Huelva cruising on the other side in hope of picking up a fare.' He would be quite happy to carry us across the Guadiana, he said – all the more as he had just been able to pick up a cheap two-stroke outboard engine able to cope with the river's strong currents following the autumn rains.

We asked whether he knew the positions of the Spanish frontier posts, to which he replied that he would not expect to stay long in business if he did not. And did many Portuguese risk crossing the frontier? 'Many,' he said. 'Many things are cheaper in Spain, so naturally people cross the river to buy them.' And the Spanish? Did they cross over, too? He shook his head. 'The girls in the cantinas here are cheaper, but they say it's easy to pick up something calling for a trip to the doctor, so the Spanish boys stay where they are.'

We sipped a harsh Portuguese sherry while our friend went through a list of attractions – many of them unique – which the Guadiana had to offer. For the most part they were only accessible to fishermen and collectors of wild-life who sometimes sneaked, armed to the teeth, across the frontier from Spain.

The Guadiana was seen locally as unique and extraordinary in every way.

'I do not expect you to do anything but cast scorn on the local belief in water-sprites,' our informant said, 'but it is remarkable how many persons of at least average education laugh and change the subject whenever it is brought up. In some areas local fishermen attempt to bribe the water-nymphs by casting edible luxuries into the river before entreating them to help with the catch. Our fishermen baptise their children without the presence of a priest who they believe would rob them of access to Almighty God.' Our friend shook his head, 'We only bring up these topics in the case of outsiders who wish to know something of our life. Above all we are conscious of the heavenly powers. You will see our fishermen at prayer before casting their lines, and every one of them bows to the river whenever a fish is caught.'

We clambered aboard and the boat took off heading south through the last of the mountain scenery where the Guadiana roared and splashed through the narrow ravines. It was to be the part of our journey that provided Eugene, as a keen amateur naturalist, with constant interest and some degree of excitement. The river's colour offered an endless variation of soft greys and greens. Bright flowers dropped by some unknown species of tree rotated like tiny wheels on the surface as they slipped by. Where the current slowed, fishermen up to their knees in water had placed themselves in the shade of every second or third tree. Curiously these fishers seemed to have disguised themselves with coolie hats like Japanese in a picture by Hiroshege. It was a scene in which little had changed for centuries.

As well as being haunted by water sprites – and slightly blurred photographs of these had appeared in the local press – the Guadiana provided curative water effective in various sicknesses and the gratitude of the community was shown by nominal libations of the best wine. What impressed us most was its marked effect on local character. The locals were cautious and premeditative in most of their activities. A fisherman, for example, might claim for a single day the right to a position among the roots of a riverside tree, but next day he moved on to a new site, not in the next tree, but the next but one. There was no such thing here as luck as we accepted it, and a permanent contest was maintained here between man's brains and those of the fish.

We were passing through a wood of tall, broad-leaved trees, claimed by the boatman to be a form of South European oak. For me the interest lay in the fact that their boughs sheltered an extraordinary population of birds, most of them vociferous members of the crow family. There were also many butterflies where the sunshine streamed through the glades. Most remarkable was the sudden vision of a densely clustered crowd of the tortoise-shell variety, under attack as they fluttered through by a number of small birds that might have been local sparrows. Two or three of these were caught while the boatman slowed down to allow us to watch, but the superior aerobatics of the butterflies in most cases permitted escape.

Although this was still Portugal at its eastern edge, the atmosphere of southern Spain soon made itself felt, and a few miles further to the east the oaks – if this they were – came to an end and the dry prairies of the European far south began.

The river's colour was a soft, almost unnatural green in which occasional sparkling reflections came and went. Nearby seasonal floodings had created a muddy depression between us and the bank, and these had been colonised by long-legged wading birds as motionless as garden statuary as they inspected their surroundings. Eugene was delighted to have discovered a golden water-lily growing there although this had been half-eaten by the birds. He spent some time in the collection of this remarkable plant.

The ferryman interrupted at this point to ask if we were ready to cross, and we climbed back into the boat and within a matter of minutes we were in Spain. It was an experience we had prepared for but which, nevertheless, took us by surprise. Less than an hour before we had been in Portugal – then familiar, but now distant and alien. Could it possibly be that even the odour of Spain was different a hundred yards from the Portuguese shore? The answer was obviously not. Yet here a peppery scent tickled the nostrils and, turning our backs on an outline of trees, we saw a village as white as an old bone in the coils of a bare mountain, behind which the sun had recently risen.

The taxi arrived as if called from a rank, driven by a Spaniard with a hard face, and the soft-faced ferryman's boat pulled away over the bright green water, into the calm trees and then out of sight. The taxi driver actually spoke English with the faint resonance of an accent picked up while working in Stoke-on-Trent.

'Do many foreigners manage to get into Spain doing it this way?' I asked him.

He laughed. 'On a good day, plenty,' he said. 'They come down here to look for a good time and even a virgin goes cheap. You can get around and enjoy yourself now we've finished with the State of Alarm.'

'How about the trouble in the Rio Tinto?'

'Nothing,' he said. 'They shot a few miners, and now they're back at work.'

I told him to take us over to one of the cafés by the water in Ayamonte and we spent a relaxed half-hour sipping *anis con sifón*. From where we sat I realised I was roughly fifty yards across a channel from Villa Real, which I had left only the night before.

'We were over there yesterday,' Eugene told him.

'I know,' he said. 'You told me. How many miles in all did you have to travel to get here the way you did it?'

'About twelve.'

'You could have paid a boatman a few hundred escudos, about a fiver, to run you over here at night.'

'It's just a question of knowing the ropes,' I said. Then I remembered the matter of the non-existence of an entry stamp in my passport.

He laughed. 'It's nothing,' he said. 'You're in Spain now.

They don't bother about these odds and ends. If you're in, you're in, and that's all that matters.'

In crossing the frontier we seemed to have left one civilisation behind and to have plunged into an entirely different one. There could have been no more complete diversity between the delicate and even withdrawn Portuguese way of life, and the hard and often bleak lifestyle Spain offered across a narrow stretch of water. The limp smiles and soft nasal voices were no more. The shoppers in the Ayamonte market, from which the bus to Seville and Cadiz set out, snapped their orders and barked their criticisms of the goods they were served. The surly, blue-jowled Spanish frontier police were in striking contrast to their simple and friendly Portuguese counterparts we had left behind.

CHAPTER 15

UNTIL THIS POINT, our experience of Spain had been largely confined to the north of the country, including such towns as San Sebastián and Pamplona, which being close to the French frontier had come inevitably under the influence of France. Apart from this we had been obliged – largely by the exigencies of the foot-slogging journey to Zaragoza – to spend a short time there to be followed by a stay in Madrid, which apart from its revolutionary fervour at the time of our visit was otherwise noted for its cosmopolitans. Andalusia, into which we now plunged, was therefore a wholly new experience.

We had become accustomed by this time to a degree of social depression, to people living in caves. But here in Andalusia, misery came into its own. Only a few miles from Ayamonte, we were to pass through settlements of windowless huts consisting of no more than holes dug in the ground with branch and straw coverings shaped like upturned boats to take the place of roofs.

Outside the first of these settlements, two blind old people quarrelling violently groped with their fingernails at each other's faces. Propped against a nearby wall was a beggar whose single leg had wasted away almost to the thinness of a finger. Obliged to stop here while the bus waited to pick up travellers, we were greeted hopefully by the poor fellow, whose act was to impart a palsied tremble to the limb for the benefit of passers-by, following this on most occasions with a howl of successful salesmanship.

Andalusia, nevertheless, was shortly to present the first of its many paradoxes. The liveliest scene in any of the small villages we passed centred on barbers' shops, around and in which the menfolk, when deprived of gainful occupation, conducted their social lives. It was socially incorrect, we were told, for Andalusian males to shave themselves, and we were assured that most self-respecting bachelors in Ayamonte visited the barbers for a shave twice a day plus a hair trim twice a week.

There was no better way of travel than by the Huelva bus rattling slowly along, with stops at a barber's every three or four hundred yards, to appreciate the only too often tragic beauty of the Spanish far south. Here the old-fashioned social conventions survived under the protection of poverty. Men still bowed low to women, acknowledged favours with hands pressed over hearts, and slipped a small coin in the sleeve of a beggar whom they addressed with the formality due to a member of the middle class.

We picked up speed and swooped through Andalusian villages that after sunset had become wholly white, and could be seen ahead glowing faintly in the sheen of the moon like a row of phosphorescent cubes set down on each side of the road. All the houses were white inside too, and then came the inescapable surprise. Although windows were covered with iron grilles like those of a feudal castle, doors were always open by way of a declaration of at least theoretical trust. Polished copper cooking untensils hung among tiny cages containing decoy partridges. But members of the household were never in sight. Under what spell had these families fallen?

At Huelva martial law was very much in evidence. The Civil Guards in their characteristic winged black hats and the newly created Assault Guards were both missing and had been replaced by a swaggering body of Marines who patrolled the streets and had occupied public buildings. Released for a half-hour or so from the bus, supposedly to allow us to stretch our legs, we joined the promenading crowds with just enough time to taste the savoury omelettes being cooked on every street corner. It was strange while engaged in this way to be startled by a brief burst of gunfire in a neighbouring street.

Returning to the bus we learnt that, after the driver's discussion with the police, it had been decided to call off the rest of the very considerable journey to Seville for that night. Accommodation was found for us in a commercial hotel where eleven travellers in the same predicament were put up in a vast single room from which a noisy caged parrot was conveniently removed.

The first wave of mass tourism had washed over Huelva only in the past few weeks and much of the surrounding area was in the process of transformation into limitless sandy beaches. This would now be renamed the Costa de la Luz, said a leaflet issued by the Tourist Board accompanying the hotel's bill. The new Costa, explained the leaflet – making the situation as clear as it could without giving local offence – would offer a solution to the problem of bringing this area of Spain up to date. There had been many instances in the past of the country being charged with failing to keep up with the times in the treatment of its visitors holidaying in the area, especially in the matter of the freedom of association of the sexes. The Costa de la Luz, concluded the leaflet, 'will take a leading role in the attraction of visitors to our country, as well as spreading the fame of a neglected earthly paradise'.

Fortunately the earthly paradise predicted for the Costa de la Luz was never likely to extend its frontiers through the shallow valleys and low, sun-dried tableland to Seville, some sixty miles away. We drove there finally in a rackety bus stuck with the tattered remnants of posters advertising a remedy for dyspepsia. It was a landscape withered at the end of a long summer, with vineyards protected by shade trees producing an abundance of small and shrivelled grapes. Grape pickers, blackened and blistered by the sun, straightened up to wave at the bus as it rattled past. There was a shortage of water here, a passenger told us, but the loneliness of imported workers used to the city life was the worst of their problems. There were stops to check tyre pressure and top up the radiator, but eventually after three hours on the road the clear profile and sparkling towers of the great southern city freed themselves from their veils of mist. Within a half-hour we were in suburbs thronged with bullock carts. Here the driver made use of a special siren to clear a passage for the bus.

We had been given the address of a rooming house overlooking the Guadalquivir. The thing was, we were told, that even forgetting the view, it offered the chance to get away from the noise. It was very cheap and the rooms were clean. A beatifically smiling small boy dashed in, trapped and killed the spiders in the corners, collected ten centavos and went off. A river boat's huge melancholic voice sounded a warning or lament as it passed below. It was followed by absolute silence apart from the swishing of the leaves in the riverside trees, and we washed and went out to find a restaurant.

The purest chance had brought us close to Seville's cathedral – largest and most splendid of Spain's numerous great churches – and this, the objective of our pilgrimage, was to be seen towering next morning in the dawn light, from among the hugger-mugger of lesser buildings crowding its walls. All accounts spoke of its grandeur and the architectural splendours it had to offer, of the *reredos* – largest in all Christianity – of the silver and bronze tombs, the great store of Goya and Murillo masterpieces, the forty-seven silver monstrances carried in the Corpus Christi procession and the much admired gift of a stuffed croco-dile presented by the Sultan of Egypt.

These were clearly the surroundings in which a member of the fairly rich and powerful Corvaja family would have sought to be entombed in anticipation of the resurrection, but we were by this time overtaken by fatigue, and it was decided to postpone the great moment of our journey's formal completion until the next day.

Here people avoided what they could of the morning heat and rose more or less at dawn, so we followed their custom and breakfasted at six and were at the cathedral's massive doors in well under the hour. In the early light the building remained silent and aloof in surroundings devoid of human activity. The nearby bushes were full of partridges which had learnt that here they were immune from the sportsmen's attack.

An hour passed before the cathedral's peons arrived on their bicycles to haul back the great outer doors, and the notice '*cerrado*' was hung on the inner ones. This was removed in another half-hour and we found ourselves in the almost barbaric splendour of the great building's interior. This came almost within an ace of the most lavish of fairground attractions, but in the struggle for ecclesiastical advertisement, good taste was never abandoned.

A swelling crescendo – a thunder almost – of organ music filled the air. A thousand lights restored the concealed brilliance of innumerable dark corners. The cathedral had been perfumed, we were assured, by five hundred arum lilies, provided in weekly instalments by a manufacturer of railroad equipment, and the bill for a splendid music system and records of sacred music imported from Germany had been picked up by the best-known of the nation's brewers of beer. We wandered past splendid statuary of the biblical martyrs and saints, and images of the three wise men gazed up at the star, twinkling in the ceiling, followed by them in their peregrination on Earth.

Later we were to compare the effect of this building upon each other. I was beginning to suspect the presence, in Eugene's case, of a Sicilian ambivalence, notable in members of his family – his father included – who while describing themselves as atheists, subjected themselves, however reluctantly, to the power of the Christian Church. Despite himself, Eugene could be described as slightly carried away, and I had not failed to notice a telltale glistening of his eye as we passed through the cathedral's doors.

There were tombs galore to be inspected, but an hour later after a careful examination of the inscriptions it had to be accepted that none bore the Corvaja name. We broached the problem with an attendant who recommended that we consult the registers. To be able to do this we would have to see the official in charge and an appointment was fixed with him for later in the day.

He proved very pleasant and eager to be helpful,

although suffering from some visual impairment which caused him difficulty with the close print of the register.

'We suffer,' he said with a brief gesture at the vast interior, 'from a chronic shortage of space, with the result that only the great monarchs of our past such as Don Alfonso El Sabio, and Don Pedro, known as The Cruel, have been given permanent resting places in the Tomb of the Kings. All those interred there in subsequent centuries have been, and will remain, permanently undisturbed.' He slightly lowered his voice to assume a conciliatory tone. 'National figures on a lesser historical scale – although, for example, famous in the literary and even financial world – might occupy a splendid sarcophagus for some twenty or thirty years. But due to what one might describe as competition for the space that remains vacant, the period of the occupation is constantly under revision. I should point out that it is not only the Corvaja family that has felt the effects of the situation.'

He took a paper from his satchel and ran his eyes over it. 'According to this report,' he said, 'the Corvajas were only confirmed as in possession of the place originally allotted for a quarter of a century, and this expired some two years ago. Several letters were sent to them, but no reply has been received to date.'

'So what has happened?' Eugene asked, and the registrar crooked his finger.

'Come with me,' he said. 'I will show you.'

We followed him as he shuffled across the nave towards a small door in the wall which he opened for brilliant sunshine to shaft through and, crossing the threshold, we found ourselves in a narrow unmade-up road running parallel with the cathedral wall. On the far side of the road a vast dry ditch contained a mountainous assortment of litter. The background to this scene was a high straggling hedge, and beyond that a seemingly empty field. We walked to the edge of the ditch for a closer inspection of its contents. These appeared for the most part to be fragments of tombstones, mixed with discarded articles of ecclesiastical furniture, some with a hardly spoiled finish, others cracked and stained or blackened by a long exposure to the elements. 'This,' said the registrar, 'is the temporary repository of tombs we have been obliged to remove.'

'Would there be any hope,' I asked, 'of unearthing an inscription, or even part of the inscription, from the Corvaja tomb?'

He shrugged his shoulders. 'Very little I'm afraid. Even if the fragments survived they are likely to be under a great weight of subsequent additions. The cathedral would do all it could to help you in your efforts but would not wish to arouse impossible hopes. There have been several attempts to recover family inscriptions but none, to the best of my knowledge, have been successful. We must remember that some tombs are now buried under tons of shattered stone and portions of them in some cases are likely to have been reduced to powder. Special machinery would be required at considerable cost to deal with the situation, and I believe in this case one should avoid holding out impossible hopes.'

I shook my head. 'That being so,' Eugene said, 'there's really nothing more to be done.'

'You could of course apply for government aid,' said the registrar. 'My feeling is that they would be sympathetic, and surely it would be worth a try. There is perhaps one drawback. The time factor. The officials involved are notoriously slow to act in such cases and might take a considerable time to reach a decision. There would certainly be a delay.'

'Of months I suppose,' I said.

He shook his head and his expression had been changed by a slow, conciliatory smile.

'No, years,' he said.

We bowed to each other and, still smiling, the registrar backed away, turned and made for the small door in the wall. I caught Eugene in a sigh. 'Not exactly the sweet taste of success,' he said, and once again his eyes glistened.

'Not exactly. All the same Ernesto will know we've done what we could for him. For all his bluster he's a philosopher at heart. A bit of a disappointment. That's all.'

Softly, through the closed door, we heard the organ begin what might have been the music of one of the psalms, and I believed it was even the psalm calling upon the believer to cast away doubt. So the tomb had now become part of the territory of legends. What of the old palace, I wondered. Doubtless, that too would have gone. But then again, perhaps it had not – and if any part of it was still there I could imagine Ernesto's joy to be sent a photograph.

We called in at a tourist office to enquire and were assured that the once-called palace would be found in one of the side-streets off the Calle Sierpes – celebrated for its serpentine wanderings among the cramped buildings of old Seville. Once in the Sierpes itself we were given more precise directions. 'It's the big shoe shop just down the road,' said our informant. We went there and spoke to the owner who made it clear that his shop was not just big, but the biggest in the province – stocking, he said, two thousand pairs of shoes.

He was a young man of great charm, who having listened

to the history of our misfortunes, immediately invited us to lunch. A narrow door opened onto a stairway spiralling up what was clearly a medieval turret in which we were to discover that a modern room had been built, and in this the meal was served. It was part of a process of renovation by which most of the palace's medieval interior had been replaced, and the new owners had benefited above all in matters of air and light. They had also been able to create, as he said, more useful space, in which stock previously stored elsewhere – amounting to roughly one thousand, five hundred pairs of shoes – could now be kept on the premises saving rental and insurance costs.

We congratulated him. What else could we do? He was a very hospitable man, and we told him how much we had enjoyed our meeting and listening to his account of the fortunes of the shoe business, and then took our leave.

'What on earth are we going to say to Ernesto?' Eugene asked.

'Tell him the truth,' I said. 'Well, more or less.'

We rang London and left a message. Ernesto came through a few minutes later. Curiously enough, his voice was clearer and his slightly broken English more comprehensible than in an ordinary conversation, as if an instrument held in his hand in some way helped to clarify and reorganise his thoughts.

'So how was the cathedral?' he asked.

'Marvellous,' I told him. 'I suppose you'd say a bit disorganised. They were getting ready for a big celebration. Everything was upside down.'

'You saw the tomb?'

'The whole area was closed off. We'll probably go back today. You'll be interested to hear we managed to see something of the old palace. Inevitably it had been left to run down.'

'They told me that,' Ernesto said.

'The Council seems to have a hand in a restoration of sorts, and a private interest was brought in.'

'It's no more than I expected,' Ernesto said. 'Municipalities don't throw money away on run-down palaces. What have they done to it?'

'It's been turned into a store.'

'What does it sell? Works of art, like most of the others?'

'This one sells shoes,' I told him. 'They call it Super Shoe – the biggest store of its kind in the province – or so they say. A Council member praised it in a speech the other day. He said it had contributed to the prosperity of Seville.'

'Has the medieval part of the building been left alone?'

'Apparently that couldn't be done. Two thousand pairs of shoes had to find a home.'

'Does anything remain of the old place as it was?' Emesto asked.

'Only the central turret. It is used for board-meetings. The Municipality agreed to the original windows being replaced by stained glass.'

'Vulgar as ever,' Ernesto said.

CHAPTER 16

AT THIS POINT in our journey both Eugene and I seemed
to be suffering from a stealthy onset of fatigue induced,
we suspected, by the long walk to Zaragoza, followed by
the over-stimulations and disappointments of the great
city. Nevertheless, far from any waning in Eugene's enthusiasm for the socialist cause, he was prepared to throw
himself once again into the struggle for justice and had
become a leader in a movement calling itself *Ayuda*. The
organisation provided assistance to foreigners in trouble
with the police, particularly adventurous young men. All
too many of them were prepared to exploit the generosity
of the local people, reminding a correspondent of the
newspaper *El Liberal* of the sturdy beggars of the Middle
Ages. These new-style villains snatched handbags, dealt in
forged banknotes, and had even kidnapped a few affluent
citizens and held them successfully for ransom. *Ayuda*
denounced juvenile offenders to the police, but only in
recognition of a bargaining system by which the severity
of police action taken against them was correspondingly
reduced.

Eugene's mistake was to describe these activities with
pride in a letter to his father. This produced nothing but
alarm and, in the hope of resuming parental control,

Ernesto took the first train to Seville, arriving two days later.

Ernesto had always claimed to have been something of a socialist himself, although, as he agreed, he was out of touch with socialism's more scientific modern form. Priming himself with a quick scan through a copy of the *Daily Worker*, and with the intention of ensuring a sympathetic reception, he presented himself at the barrier of the Seville railway station with a red rosette in his lapel and his fist raised in a communist salute. The ticket collector alerted a Civil Guard lurking nearby, and Ernesto found himself under arrest. A brief questioning followed before he was released with an exchange of apologies and smiles and the police delivered him to our hotel.

We had received no warning that Ernesto was on his way, and it was therefore to our amazement that while loitering in a somewhat dishevelled lane we should suddenly be confronted by this amazing old Sicilian, dressed as he might have been for a stroll in the Strada Duca di Urbino, Palermo, with his somewhat outdated spats, eye-shade and a malacca cane with which he swiped off the tops of weeds. A bowler hat completed his costume. This, we were later assured, was not the hat in which the entrails of his friend had been collected on the occasion of the perilous duel, but a recent replacement.

The Sacramento Hotel benefited from the foresight of its owners in arranging its construction roughly within three hundred yards of the cathedral of which, from a slight eminence, it provided an exceptional view. In addition it offered special full-board rates to pilgrims, most of whom were notoriously short of cash.

It turned out that Ernesto had been a regular guest of

the hotel. 'It's a place where you live in the past,' he said, insisting that we should make the climb up to the nineteenth-century verandah. 'You can't match the view. Nothing's been touched here for a hundred years. The only reason they leave things alone is because they can't afford to do otherwise.' The great feature of the view was inevitably the majestic profile of the cathedral, and an elegantly scripted notice supplied a list of the features of one of the three greatest churches in the Christian world.

Mention was also made of the entombment here of Spain's most terrible kings, including Don Pedro the Cruel, who lay almost side by side with the most famous citizen in the nation's history, Christopher Columbus. In the subsequent contest for burial space purchase prices were based on the affordable proximity to one or other of these magnificent sepulchres, a pseudo-magical power being believed to leak into the surrounding tombs. Ernesto told us of a prosperous tallow-candle merchant of his acquaintance who spent thirty years of his life writing an account of the religious problems leading to the Seven Years War. His remains had subsequently been accommodated in the much sought-after Don Pedro area. No space, he said, would have been available at any price in the Columbus zone for a half-century.

There could have been no better day for gazing at the view of the cathedral from the hotel verandah, for suddenly, in the mid-afternoon, and without the slightest warning, a south wind from the Gulf swept an immense number of sea birds into the sky, and one of these, identified by Eugene as a pelican, had alighted on a finial of the Giralda tower.

The extraordinary presence of this large and somewhat unwieldy bird, known only as a native of the Gulf of Cadiz, perched on the topmost point of the highest building in this part of Spain, appeared even to Ernesto as a phenomenon devoid of rational explanation. Although an abstemious man who did his best to keep his wits about him when faced with puzzles familiar in southern climes, he was driven on this occasion to steady his thinking with the aid of a glass of potent local wine. Later in the day, explanations were forthcoming. The pelican, said an early edition of the *ABC*, was constantly mistaking the green enamel sprayed over the wrought iron, often employed on the facades of government buildings, for edible foliage. The small crowds who gathered in the cathedral square watched the spectacle with amazement and then derision until the bird was finally blown away by strong winds. For some, however, the bird's presence was immediately accepted as a possibly dangerous omen and the more superstitious peasants in the vicinity burnt offerings in their houses.

The incident prompted discussion regarding the purpose of our own visit. The question Ernesto now asked himself was whether the Corvajas' pilgrimages to Spain were any more rational than a pelican's flight from the swamps? Had not the time come for normal human beings to reject the servilities inherited from the past? Was it not pride in its most absurd form to be able to claim that one's grandfather's tomb was a few metres from the sarcophagus of Pedro the Cruel? Now even that doubtful privilege was not the case.

'Do we have to bother about these things?' Eugene wanted to know.

'Of course we don't,' Ernesto said. 'I think our pilgrimages should end and we'll return to London.'

CHAPTER 17

IT MUST HAVE been evident to Ernesto within minutes of his happy reunion with his son that only the softest and subtlest approach to the problem of persuading Eugene to return home to England was likely to prove successful. By no possible interpretation of the word socialism could it have been alleged that Ernesto was in the slightest concerned with bettering the condition of the poor, or the problems of those in trouble with the law. Nevertheless his appreciation of the troubles involved at times of financial crisis in general was vast and varied. Was this an occasion when the power of money could be put to better use than it so often was?

Ayuda's survival was dependent on successful financing and Ernesto was convinced that what otherwise threatened to become a family problem could almost certainly be handled with the aid of a gambling syndicate with whom he had conducted mutually satisfactory business in the past.

'You talk of raising money, Father,' Eugene said, 'but how? You mean here? In Seville?'

'Absolutely not,' Ernesto told him. 'They don't go in for charity here. Surely you know that. Only the priests get fat. To get a charity going of the kind you have in mind you'd have to do it from England. I could talk to a friend in one of the gambling syndicates who'd probably help.'

'And you think there's some hope they'll agree?'

'I think we might be able to put together some sort of a case. I've helped them out once or twice and they'd probably lend a friendly ear to what I had to say.'

'That would be great.'

'Here you're a foreigner,' Ernesto emphasised. 'They don't understand the workings of your mind, and therefore they mistrust you. The project as you have described it could go down fairly well back in England just because it's the kind of exotic, slightly romantic thing that appeals to people who on the whole live dull lives.'

Soon after Ernesto's arrival, I began to detect a mild attack of nerves spreading through the city. Within twenty-four hours of the first whispers of the words 'Civil War', people began preparing for the worst. Hawkers appeared on the streets selling first-aid kits containing bandages, ointments and a miscellany of surgical odds and ends. These included crutches and even a recent invention in the form of a small tool with antiseptic cream in its handle supposedly useful in emergency extractions of bullets. In a matter of days calendars had appeared in the street markets printed with double the usual number of non-auspicious days. Regular fortune-tellers operating in the markets had switched from small-scale personal happenings to prophecies concerned with the coming war.

Ernesto was in the hotel, playing with the dogs. He had got over the long journey by this time and I had rarely seen him more relaxed. 'Did you happen to read your *ABC* today?' I asked.

'I got as far as the headlines. They're good because at least they save time. Whether they know it or not they also tell you what not to believe, although it's far from the intention.'

'Did you read the story about the coming civil war?' I asked him. 'Do you really think it could happen?'

'Let's put it this way. I can't think of any country in Europe where the likelihood is greater.'

Eugene arrived to join in the discussion with a typical left-wing point of view. 'Is this anything to do with the workers' struggle against bourgeois exploitation?' he asked, and Ernesto shook his head.

'No,' he said. 'It will be due to a loss of discipline among all classes. They are determined to fight each other. The Monarchists will be at the throats of the Liberal Republicans. The Reds will assassinate the Monarchists and vice versa. That will leave no one to be killed except those belonging to no political party who will naturally murder each other – even with no excuse. I hate to tell you this,' the old man said, 'but civil war is the only possibility. Did you read something in yesterday's *ABC* about Franco? He was reported to have been seen within a mile of where we are sitting now. All the papers call him *El Caudillo*, which means The Boss. He comes here because they have the best riding horses, and he's given out that he was christened in the cathedral – which isn't true. If Franco takes over the Army he will bring the Moors in from Morocco.'

'Just a moment,' I said. 'Does he speak Arabic?'

'Better than most speak Spanish. In North Africa he's already accepted as a mullah. All the Moroccan troops will be on his side. The day he's accepted as Caudillo in Spain, the civil war is on.'

'After what you have just told us, do you hold out any hope for Spain?'

'Yes!' Eugene broke in. 'International volunteers from Britain, France, perhaps even Germany. They will come to defend democracy.'

The prospect of war was seen by most Spaniards as a national tragedy. It revealed itself in a sense of dread that could be postponed but never wholly banished from the mind. If Seville believed in the probability of conflict, that was enough. The time had come for Spaniards to brace themselves for the inevitable battles. Seville cast its mind back to the wars of the past and its citizens – or rather those that could afford to do so – began to turn their houses into little fortresses with steel shutters over the windows and concrete reinforcement of the walls. Some house-holders employed guards who invariably wore peaked caps to provide a somewhat official appearance, although they in fact looked little different to tramcar conductors – or even the exceptionally belligerent Assault Guards.

By protecting their houses the owners appeared only to increase their fears. People removed hidden weapons from their hiding places, loaded them, and were ready when the first shots were fired.

For a moment, however, the possibility of war was put out of Ernesto's mind and discussions shifted to arrange-ments for returning home. Something was said laughingly about not having been able to do what we had set out to do, but the subject was awkwardly changed, although not before someone had blundered in with a reference to the unvisited tomb.

Incredibly enough, it was at this point, and to general astonishment, that what might well have been a fragment of the tomb was unearthed by a digger at work in the dry ditch behind the cathedral and sent on to us. It was brought to the hotel by a sacristan for our inspection. The chip was of clean, white marble, about four inches in length. The sacristan made a point of telling us that a number of such fragments had been recovered, all quite small and most somewhat stained. Ernesto was fetched to examine it and it was mooted that perhaps possession of a variety of such fragments might be reasonably acceptable as a symbolic visit to the tomb in its entirety.

There was something in Eugene's manner at about this time to suggest that he was ill at ease. I would have been happy to return home without further delay, but my feeling was that he was in no hurry to do so.

'Do you really like it here?' he wanted to know, but I may have shown insufficient enthusiasm in my reply. When he came back to the subject I told him that I had preferred Madrid.

'Didn't you object to having to hold your hands up when we went for a stroll?'

'It was all right if you didn't have far to go. That is to say, apart from crossing the Gran Via on one's hands and knees.'

'I could have done without it,' Eugene said. 'Anyway, how about Seville? Do you like Seville?'

'I know I shouldn't admit to it, but as a matter of fact I do, I think it has a soul.'

'I didn't realise you're a bible-buster after all,' Eugene said.

'Sorry,' I said. 'It's my Welsh upbringing. A tabernacle supper with poached eggs on Saturday nights. It leaves its mark. Still, all the same, you've managed to give Ernesto a case of nerves. He's already checking on the trains. A Paris Express leaves the day after tomorrow.'

'It's all the same to me,' Eugene said. 'I'm ready to go whenever you like.'

'But I'm not sure I believe you,' I told him.

'Well, you'll see for yourself,' he said. For a moment he seemed absorbed in thought, and when he spoke again it was with a change of tone. 'If a real war breaks out here, I'll come back.'

'What on earth for?' I asked him.

'To fight against the fascists,' he said.

'And you believe there'll be one?'

'I'm almost certain there will,' he told me, and I could see he meant it. Further discussion was almost incredibly interrupted by the return of the mounted *requetes*, this time having apparently doubled the number we had seen on the occasion of their earlier patrol. But what was to startle us most was the spectacle of a countryman, his arms roped behind him, being dragged at the tail of the last horse. 'This,' Eugene said, 'must be what *El Debate* meant yesterday when it spoke of the necessity of establishing new disciplines.'

'And what is that supposed to mean?' I asked.

'Usually what the Americans used to call lynch law. If you were unlucky enough to fall out with one of the bosses you got beaten up and thrown into the river.'

'And you think they could get away with that here?'

'Probably. The system worked well in Italy. They have just as many fascists round Seville now as there were there. They've even invented a fascist salute. You pat the inner muscles of your right arm and hold up your hand,' Eugene explained.

'Shouldn't you tell Ernesto about this?' I urged. 'If we have to go home in any case surely we ought to make a move before the new fascists get busy. Otherwise we may find ourselves stuck here until further notice. In any case, I believe he intends to settle for the Paris Express.'

'It's all the same to me,' Eugene said. 'I'll be travelling with you on the train.'

CHAPTER 18

THE FIRST IMPRESSION of the train on which we were about to travel northwards through Spain was that it had captured and retained a little of the vivacity of the streets of Seville – to say nothing of their homely odours. Passengers were burdened with immense packages (one had arrived with a small dog wrapped up like a parcel), and a large but fragile box had split open to release a shower of miscellaneous objects including a selection of feminine underwear. Having settled, the passengers pursued every form of activity compatible with the journey. A painter of 'three-minute portraits' had secured a corner in which to work and set up an easel next to a priest guarding a pile of missals in ragged-edged covers. Innumerable small children were being pacified by bribery or threats. A fighting cock, fitted with a shining spur, had been crammed into a cage from which it continued a strangled outcry. The odour, apart from that of humanity forced into over-small space, was of ripe cheeses. Despite the stresses of such international journeys, the travellers had clearly set out to be affable, and it was evident that a high standard of good humour would be maintained.

But it was to be a long journey and the first few miles

of the almost empty spread of the Andalusian outback under a long drawn-out high noon threatened monotony. Time passed, and at last there were splendid views for the traveller to enjoy. Enormous swamps had been created by the rainstorms that had burst the banks of the Guadalquivir. Charred stacks remained of a village fired by lightning. Mountains with labyrinthine caves were yet to be explored, and the small town of Campobello had warning signs painted in yellow on the walls to signify that it had been visited by the plague. Best of all, with their offering of limitless interest, were the forests and lakes filling the long terrestrial depression that joins Seville to Cordoba and few such areas of Spain were likely to keep the traveller so ardently awake.

Dawn reorganised sprawling torsos and straightened cramped limbs, except in the case of Ernesto, who had stayed awake, reading the *Meditations* of Marcus Aurelius. Daybreak spread like a slow conflagration into all corners of the landscape. The black smoke of morning fires twisted into the sky, unchained dogs hurled themselves against invisible intruders, and a peasant defecated beneath a flight of partridges in search of mountain hiding places.

Eugene and I studied our maps. Somewhere in the vicinity – give or take a dozen miles – the railway track, avoiding the hills, ravines and forests which turned day into night, curved away between the Pyrenees and the sea towards San Sebastián.

'We'll be calling in there for the last time, I imagine, and putting up at the Royalty?' I said.

'If they have rooms, why not?' Eugene said. 'Be nice to see Dorotea again, if she still works there.'

'And even take a last stroll on the *paseo* with her, and

a suitable friend if she happens to have one. We have to take flowers for Dorotea, whatever we do.'

An English-speaking passenger had overheard us and was keen to help. 'No problem at all, sir. For Miss Dorotea flowers of all kinds are sold at railway station. In five spare minutes also, if you wish these people will make small poem and personal message for accompanying flowers. As fellow traveller, sir, I wish you success.'

The Paris Express, living up to its reputation, was on time to the dot at San Sebastián. The station counter was banked with exotic blossoms, and a telephone call revealed that Dorotea was still at her place of work. She said she would be delighted to see us again, adding that by a miraculous chance that particular afternoon happened to be free. It would be nice for us, she thought, to take in what was generally described as the splendid flower show at the park, and we were naturally equally enthusiastic. The meeting, however, after a short taxi ride to the show, had something about it that smelt of confrontation, confirming a suspicion that Ernesto was concerned only with our prompt and uninterrupted return to the United Kingdom. There was something in his brief conversation with Dorotea that seemed to conceal frigidity behind a token politeness.

At this moment a new complication arose. A messenger sent after us from the hotel presented us with a letter from a London newspaper that said, to Eugene's amazement, that it had accepted two of his travel pieces and – even more to his surprise – expressed moderate interest in a description of the local *paseo*, which had apparently attracted a number of English visitors to San Sebastián. Mastering his fury, Ernesto was obliged to accept a delay in our departure. Dorotea bought a new dress and organised our inclusion in the parade, and Ernesto shut himself in his room and settled down to read biblical passages in archaic Spanish.

'Please excuse me,' he said. 'I'm turning my back on modern times.'

CHAPTER 19

THE FINAL LEG of our journey back to England, by ship, had been arranged through a Spanish tourist agency at extremely low rates, and they had warned of possible uncertainties awaiting us. We were greeted with almost excessive affability by the ship's officers lined up at the top of the gangplank, and a substantial bouquet of flowers did something to mitigate the austerity of our cabin. Remote rumbles and gruntings proclaimed the engine had started. Very shortly afterwards we were asked to attend lifeboat drill, and the chance of rough weather ahead was hinted at.

Eugene suddenly broke into my thoughts, and I realised that something was the matter.

'I need a drink,' he said. 'I've done the wrong thing.'

'What's bothering you?' I asked him. 'Everything has gone off all right so far.'

'I've let myself down.'

'I don't understand you.'

'I realise now I should have stayed.'

'What on earth for?'

'I want to get back on good terms with my conscience.'

'Is this something to do with the Civil War?'

'I'm afraid it is,' Eugene said.

'I realise how you feel,' I told him, 'but for all that you should wait for the right moment.'

'This is it. Did you see the headline in that Spanish rag *Debate*, about soldiers of fortune flooding into Spain?'

'I read it but I didn't necessarily believe it. *Debate* is a fascist paper.'

'It's common knowledge that Franco has been enlisting mercenaries to take on any who turn out to be left-wingers.'

'Don't let's delude ourselves. Mercenaries or not, they'll put up a fight.'

'A gang of thugs,' Eugene said. 'We'd make mincemeat of them.'

I saw him as just too certain of victory. There were times when his brand of optimism appeared to me almost as a weakness.

'Think it over,' I said. 'Think about it before you commit yourself to something you may come to regret.'

Once back in London, it soon became clear to Ernesto that Eugene was keen to continue his involvement with his beloved *Ayuda* project. He and I were both on the lookout for jobs. We hadn't seen each other for some time when I had a call from Eugene.

'I've decided I'm going back to Spain.' There seemed to be relief in his voice.

'Why? When?'

'It's a touchy situation. I'm anxious to get over there while the going is still good. Nobody knows exactly what's likely to happen next. The offer came for me to go, and the thing is not to hang about, but to grab the opportunity while I can.'

'Well, I wish you the very best of luck. I hope I'll see you before you go, and keep in touch.'

'As they say, *venceremos*. We're going to win. Join us if you can.'

POSTSCRIPT

AT ABOUT THIS time, the modestly left-wing caretaker government of Largo Caballero, convinced of the hopelessness of defending Madrid from attack by the fascist leader General Franco, lost face by deserting the historic site of the capital in favour of Valencia on the coast. Inevitably the fascist regimes of Germany and Italy were behind Franco, but at least no efforts were made by democratic governments to prevent their nationals from joining International Brigades.

Franco's German allies were called in to devastate the ancient Basque town of Guernica, while Italian troops were imported to massacre Spanish peasants regarded as a result of their poverty as 'left wing'. Indignity was piled upon our Spanish friends in Seville, where Moroccan mercenaries massacred more peasants in the countryside and German soldiers of fortune invaded the city itself. An attack by German warplanes in this area was reported to have caused the loss of 30,000 lives. It was estimated that a further 30,000 casualties were suffered by random though persistent attack, largely by foreign planes, in the Ebro valley.

Eugene was among the first from England to enlist in the International Brigades, but it came as no surprise that he would do so only as an ambulance driver – which he remained until the withdrawal of his brigade in November 1938. He had been lucky enough to escape being wounded, but he had suffered ill-health through periods of semi-starvation throughout the campaign, and it was this that abruptly shortened his life.

ABOUT THE AUTHOR

NORMAN LEWIS'S EARLY childhood was spent partly with his Welsh spiritualist parents in Enfield, North London, and partly with his eccentric aunts in Wales. Forgoing a place at university for lack of funds, he used the income from wedding photography and various petty trading to finance travels to Spain, Italy, and the Balkans, before being approached by the British Colonial Office to spy for them with his camera in Yemen.

He moved to Cuba in 1939, but was recalled for duty in the Intelligence Corps during the Second World War. It was from this that Norman Lewis's masterpiece, *Naples'44*, emerged, a resurrection of his wartime diary only finally published in 1978.

Before that came a number of novels and travel books, notably A *Dragon Apparent* (1951) and *Golden Earth* (1952), both of which were best sellers in their day. His novel The *Volcanoes Above Us*, based on personal experiences in Central America, sold six million copies in paperback in Russia and *The Honoured Society* (1964), a nonfiction study of the Sicilian Mafia, was serialized in six installments by the *New Yorker*.

Norman Lewis was the author of thirteen novels and thirteen works of nonfiction, mostly travel books, but he regarded his life's major achievement to be the reaction to an article written by him entitled "Genocide in Brazil," published in the *Sunday Times* in 1968. This led to a change in the Brazilian law relating to the treatment of Indians, and to the formation of Survival International, the influential international organization which campaigns for the rights of tribal peoples.

More recent books included *Voices of the Old Sea* (1984), *Goddess in the Stones: Travels in India* (1991), *An Empire of the East: Travels in Indonesia* (1993), *The World, the World* (1996), which concluded his autobiography, as well as collections of pieces in *The Happy Ant Heap* (1998) and *Voyage by Dhow* (2001). With In *Sicily* (2002) he returned to his much-loved Italy.

Norman Lewis died in 2003 at the age of ninety-three after completing *The Tomb in Seville*, this account of his 1934 journey through Spain and Portugal.

NAPLES '44:

A World War II Diary of Occupied Italy

From the author Graham Greene
called "one of our best writers,
not of any particular decade
but of our century," comes a
masterpiece about a war-ravaged
city under occupation

AS A YOUNG INTELLIGENCE OFFICER stationed in a stunned and bleeding Naples following its liberation from Nazi forces, Norman Lewis recorded the lives of a proud and vibrant people forced to survive on prostitution, thievery, and a desperate belief in miracles and cures. The most popular of Lewis's books, *Naples '44* is a landmark poetic study of the agony of wartime occupation and its ability to bring out the worst, and often the best, in human nature. In prose both heartrending and comic, Lewis describes an era of disillusionment, escapism, and hysteria in which the Allied occupiers mete out justice unfairly and fail to provide basic necessities to the populace while Neapolitan citizens accuse each other of being Nazi spies, women offer their bodies to the same Allied soldiers whose supplies they steal to sell on the black market, and angry young men organize militias to oppose "temporary" foreign rule. Yet over the chaotic din, Lewis sings intimately of the essential dignity of the Neapolitan people whose civility, courage, and generosity of spirit shine through daily.

"Vivid, lucid, eloquent, often funny, more often bitter and melancholy . . . [An] elegantly written little book." —*New York Times Book Review*

"Norman Lewis is one of the greatest twentieth century British writers and *Naples '44* is his masterpiece. A lyrical, ironic and detached account of a tempestuous, byzantine and opaque city in the aftermath of war." —Will Self

"A Goya, powerful and bizarre." —*Saturday Review*

Carroll & Graf Publishers / 192 pages / ISBN 0-7867-1438-7 / $13.95 / 2005
Available from all chain, independent, and online booksellers